The Metropolitan Story

Patrick R. Foster

Published by

**krause
publications**

700 E. State Street • Iola, WI 54990-0001
Telephone: 715/445-2214

Please call or write for our free catalog of automotive publications. Our toll-free number to place an order or obtain a free catalog is 800-258-0929 or please use our regular business telephone 715-445-2214 for editorial comment and further information.

Library of Congress Catalog Number: 96-766688
ISBN: 0-87341-459-4
Printed in the United States of America

Dedication

This book is dedicated to the men and women of Nash-Kelvinator Corporation for the noble work and wonderful products they and that fine old company produced. Nash truly was one the greatest of the American independent automakers (and some would argue the greatest) and we applaud the splendid contribution that all of you hard working folks made to automotive history. God Bless you all!

Contents

THE METROPOLITAN STORY

BY PATRICK R. FOSTER
With Karl Harris

This lovely young lady proudly poses with her Met convertible.

Foreword

It's a funny thing about Americans. We believe ourselves to be an open-minded people and yet in order for small cars to finally begin to take hold in the U.S. market in the 1950s, our supposedly unclosed minds had to be forcefully pried open through the efforts of a few dedicated individuals. These persons came primarily from the ranks of the independent automobile makers; those smaller producers who sold cars principally in the medium price segment, or focused on a narrow market niche at the bottom of the price range. For some of these companies, the small car market proved to be a decidedly unfriendly terrain: witness Hudson, Crosley, and Kaiser's Henry J.

But not so for Nash-Kelvinator. That company seemed to understand that, in the beginning at least, a small car had to be marketed as a special automobile, a classy item, a smart car for chic people. Nash sensed that to be successful, a small car had to be sold on more than just a low price tag. After all, any automobile with a reputation as being a poor person's car would probably be shunned even by poor people, wouldn't it? Does anyone remember the Yugo?

But then, those other automobile companies lacked a vital asset that couldn't be duplicated; they didn't have George Mason as CEO. Mason was as brilliant an automobile man as ever lived, honest and smart, a tough trader but a fair one and yet a genuinely warm and friendly human being. He was revered by his dealers and beloved by his co-workers. We remember him nowadays with respect equally for his outstanding character as well as for his great accomplishments.

The Metropolitan Story is more than simply a narrative about great cars; it is also a tale about great men; George Mason, George Romney and others. It is a story of how a modest sized company was able to crack the small car market in America with perhaps the cleverest little car of all time.

When I first brought up my idea for an American Motors trilogy, people in the business looked at me as if I were from another planet. "An AMC trilogy?," they asked, "is that possible?" Now, three years since *American Motors The Last Independent* was published, this second book in the series is here for your enjoyment and yes, I still think it's possible.

But don't credit only me for it. The truth is there's one person who more than anyone else made this book possible and that's Karl Harris, Met enthusiast, Rambler aficionado and co-author. Karl was the spark plug that got the idea moving and without his help this story might not have been published. Thanks, too, should be lavishly showered on the wonderful Pat Klug, of Krause Publications, for her support of the project. Ms. Klug has been a good friend to the AMC hobby.

Several significant others lent their support and I'd like to recognize them here: Paul Lehman of Class Action Videos (which produces an excellent Metropolitan video), Diana Hawkinson, Guy Hadsall (a wonderful man and former manager of shows and exhibits at AMC), Rich McGarty of the *Met Gazette*, AMC hobbyist Chris Zinn, former Miss America Evelyn Ay Sempier, retired Nash and AMC designer Bill Reddig, (who's one of the nicest people God ever created), and retired independent designer Bill Flajole, the father of the Metropolitan. Thanks also go to the remarkable former Nash and AMC engineer Carl Chakmakian, and the warm and generous Roy D. Chapin Jr., former Chairman of the Board of American Motors Corporation.

Several others who have since passed away were helpful and you should know about them: a man I've long admired, George Romney, former Nash Executive Vice-President, AMC Chairman and former Governor of Michigan, my old friend former Nash and AMC Styling Director Ed Anderson, and former Metropolitan Sales Manager James Watson.

I'd like to thank my lovely wife, Diane, for having the patience of a saint and for implicitly acknowledging the importance of the work I do by allowing me the time and space to do it, and my daughter Caitlin, for being such a source of joy to me. Thanks too, to two great photographers, W. Scott Cameron and Victor Miller. Thanks also to the Society of Automotive Historians, Dr. Bob, without whom I might not be here, David Austin for his Metropolitan Chronology, Will Fox and Frank Peiler of *Collectible Automobile* magazine and to all the unsung members of the Metropolitan Club, the Nash Club, the American Motors Owners Club, the AMC Rambler Club, AMC World Clubs, the Pacer Club and the Hudson Club, for their support for my first book and this one.

Special recognition should go to John A. Conde, the dean of American Motors historians and authors, whose work has inspired so many others to follow in his footsteps.

Here, then, is the story of a truly warm and wonderful car, the fabulous decade it appeared in, the people who designed it, the folks who built it, the salesmen who sold it and the wonderful men and women who bought the cars and loved them and who cherish them still. So find yourself a comfy chair, put on a pair of slippers and fix yourself a nice cup of tea. This is a story you'll want to savor.

Author Patrick Foster. (Photo courtesy of Victor Miller)

A Word About The Photographs Used in This Book

One thing you'll notice in *The Metropolitan Story* is the lavish array of photos used. The greatest percentage of photos came from two primary sources, the collection of Karl Harris, and the Patrick R Foster Collection. Many other folks were kind enough to donate photos to this effort, however. We'd like to thank Evelyn Ay Sempier, Bill Reddig, Guy Hadsall, Paul Lehman, Diana Hawkinson, John A. Conde, Peter Marshall, Chris Zinn, Jimmy Valentine, Nick Georgano, *Collectible Automobile* magazine and all the Met owners whose pictures appear within.

Chapter One

The Most Wonderful Car in the World

It was a revolution on wheels; it was pure automotive whimsy. It was the perfect car for the young and carefree, and for the stylish, chic and smart. *American Motors* called it the Metropolitan. It was a car that made good sense for frugal motorists and yet was great fun for career girls on the go. Writer Devon Francis said it was a "watch charm Rolls-Royce." Some folks referred to it as an English Rambler, which of course it really wasn't, and a multitude of others simply failed to understand its place in American culture. There were all sorts of rumors and foolishness associated with the Met, the root stock from which myths and legends grow. A few souls, bless their na-

ive little hearts, even believed it was amphibious; others believed it could go 80 miles on a gallon of gas, but of course neither of these ideas was true.

And yet, it was a machine of compelling interest. Stated at its very essence, the Metropolitan was a new type of American automobile, unusually small for its market and its era, built in England yet designed and engineered in the United States for use on American roads by American drivers. It was sold and serviced in this country by Nash, Hudson and American Motors dealers.

It was one of the first cars whose marketing was clearly aimed at women, and as such it reflected the ma-

Any Metropolitan owner can tell you, it's a wonderful car!

Is this Met smiling?

jor social changes that occurred in this country after World War II. Thus, the Metropolitan can be viewed as perky and pretty, and socially significant too.

It's also, as any owner will inform you, The Most Wonderful Car in the World.

The Metropolitan was not the Car of Kings, but it could be called the Car of Queens. Miss America for 1954, Evelyn Ay of Lancaster, Pennsylvania, helped introduce the Metropolitan to America. She recalls that experience for us later in this book. Princess Margaret of England was an enthusiastic Metropolitan owner. Oh, yes, and royalty inspired the production of a handful of custom Mets, each of which was called a Royal Runabout. That's quite a story in itself, which we cover later on.

Throughout its nine year run, the tiny Met endeared itself to TV, film and theater personalities. Actress Ann Southern reportedly was a Met owner, so was TV star John Bromfield, as well as several financial news colum-

The owner of this Metropolitan modified it with tailfins!

nists, some well-known automobile writers, a beautiful and talented water ski ballerina, several police departments, a clown, a few radio station and newspaper fleets, a tin pan alley song writer, two press photographers, an enthusiastic priest and nearly 100,000 "ordinary" others, all in love with the Metropolitan. AMC Chairman George Romney even tried to sell one to Prescott Bush, father of future president George Bush.

How popular are Metropolitans today? Well, a clean used Met can easily fetch several times the price it sold for new. Even so, the tiny Brit remains one of the more affordable collector cars and certainly one of the most distinctive. As one enthusiast noted, "When you own a Metropolitan, you never lack for conversation. Strangers approach at every opportunity, anxious to see and touch your little dream machine." To see a Met is to love a Met!

Metropolitan police car.

That explains the reaction most people have when they see a Met drive up. Everybody stares in bemused surprise, then smiles begin to appear on faces and fond memories are recalled. Old cars have a way of doing that to people, but the Metropolitan is the world's champion in that regard. Nobody can ignore a Metropolitan, yet because of its cute, friendly looks, it's one car that's never intimidating. Strangers think nothing of walking up and starting a conversation with a Met owner. This is without a doubt the most lovable car you can own.

Join us now as we take a walk through the history of this unique and wonderful car. Along the way we'll see the Met that Paul Newman and Joanne Woodward once owned, talk with the designers of the Metropolitan, meet some of the far-sighted executives who pushed the idea of a small car for ladies (and gentlemen), and look at some of the prettiest automobiles you've ever seen. As an extra treat, many of the exciting pictures you'll view have never before been published. So come now as we take a look at this revolution in culture and cars.

This Met took its owner to see America's capital.

IN THE BEGINNING:

In retrospect, it's easy to see that what happened was simply inevitable. As the old saying goes, "how can you keep them on the farm once they've been to Paris?"

A revolution was coming and it involved a changing culture and a new type of automobile. In the years before World War II, the automobile in America was primarily a masculine device. Most early automobile buyers and users were male. It's true there were many women driving, but they were in a minority and were locked in a culture that defined their roles and activities primarily in a domestic context. Most women lived in cities where travel to the butcher, baker and general store could be achieved by walking, use of a trolley or simply by waiting for the man of the house to drive them. Relatively few women worked outside the home and thus few earned an income. These two facts meant that few women had an overpowering need for an automobile. Cars were designed primarily for men, though admittedly colors and interior fabrics were often designed to appeal to the distaff side of the household.

Things began to change during World War II. As men were called up to serve in the armed forces and war factories went to round-the-clock production shifts, shortages in the work force became a major problem. In Washington, D.C., terse Senate hearings addressed rumors of "labor hoarding" in certain industries. Industrial planners spent countless hours searching for workers for assembly lines that were stretched to capacity.

America's women stepped up to the challenge. "We Can Do It" became a rallying cry. Give us training, give

One of America's truly great automotive leaders, George W. Mason of Nash-Kelvinator.

us tools and give us a chance, they said, and for the sake of democracy, America listened. Thus was born "Rosie the Riveter," a symbol of American determination in the face of total war. American women helped boost production of war materiel to unheard-of levels.

At war's end many of those female workers settled back to domestic life. But some didn't, deciding instead to remain in the workforce. Even those who chose to return to household duties ended up starting a revolution in the housing market by migrating with their families to new communities being built on the outskirts of cities. Since these communities were not within urban limits yet were not far out enough to be considered rural, they became known by a new term: sub-urban, or suburban if you prefer. The Burbs.

This combination of a skilled, wage-earning womanhood, when added to the more conventional-minded women living in suburban areas far from stores, meant that a new market segment would soon emerge, a market of women drivers independent enough to desire a car different from what their husbands, fathers, boyfriends or brothers had.

In addition, there was a vocal segment of the market expressing a desire for small sporty cars. Americans had come into contact with sports cars during wartime European service. Upon returning home, they formed the nucleus of a new market niche for such cars. Sales volumes were tiny but growing and, for all Detroit knew, it might end up being a significant market.

Few in the auto industry saw the change coming and only one man decided to focus his company's efforts toward serving the new market. It's not by coincidence that he is considered by many to have been one of the most visionary, influential and important automobile men of all time, George W. Mason, chairman of Nash-Kelvinator.

Mason had the physical appearance of a comfortable old-line auto man, large bodied with stubby fingers usually grasping a fat cigar, face customarily wearing the easy smile of a natural born salesman. None of this was meant to be deceptive; he was a happy man who enjoyed fine dining, and it showed. He enjoyed good cigars as well, and it's easier to locate photographs of him with his stogies than without. But his physical appearance did not reflect a sedentary lifestyle. Quite the contrary; Mason enjoyed duck hunting, loved trout fishing and played an occasional game of golf as well. More importantly, he was not satisfied with his company's position and place in the market. He wanted Nash-Kelvinator to grow. To George Mason, business was a long-term, high stakes contest, one to be played boldly or not at all.

He chose to be bold. Mason was possessed of rare business vision, far reaching and of immense clarity, and in this regard he far surpassed his contemporaries. He looked into the future of the automobile industry and saw things few others did. He saw the new women's market coming; the population shifting away from cities; he saw an upcoming change in driving habits; and he knew that the postwar era could bring unsurpassed prosperity to the nation. He also saw inflation, higher wage costs, much higher tooling costs and, inevitably, much higher costs for automobiles.

He decided on a multi-faceted plan to meet the new world head on. In the immediate postwar period, he would offer warmed-over versions of the prewar Nash. The design, after all, had been all-new in 1941 and was still fresh and modern. The lower priced series, the Nash 600, had debuted a type of body construction relatively new to America, "unitized" or unibody design. It eliminated the regular frame, replacing it with a body structure that welded the floor, sides and roof together for increased strength and lower weight. Mason wanted Nash products to offer unique features not available on other American cars and he knew unibody was a tremendously important product advantage.

Mason also knew that the pent-up demand for new cars, created when war production forced the industry to halt car production from early 1942 to mid 1945, would keep assembly lines hard at work for several years. Thus, he planned to wait until 1949 to introduce a completely new car. In the meantime he set his engineers, designers and product planners to work designing innovative new products for the decade that would be dawning just as the pent-up demand was being sated: the fifties.

Nash's Experimental Motorized Bicycle was one of the early "Minimum Transportation" devices that Nash tested in search for low-cost transportation for the public. (l-r) George Romney; Fred L. Black, public relations director; George Mason; B. B. Geyer, advertising executive; Edmund E. Anderson, Director of Styling; and an unidentified gentleman.

Earlier studies by the Automobile Manufacturers Association (AMA) had developed some interesting information. Automobile usage had gradually shifted away from long distance pleasure/vacation travel and was now primarily short distance, around-town use. Most of the industry gave that little thought, but to Mason the studies, combined with the other factors, pointed toward a possible market for cars that were smaller than the average or so-called "standard size" American car. His product planners and engineers began investigating various "minimum transportation" designs, according to company statements, as early as 1943. They were looking for an ideal "light" vehicle, one that would represent the minimum size that most Americans would find acceptable. The Nash experimental garage soon became home to perhaps the oddest assortment of mini vehicles ever assembled by an independent auto company. Mason wanted to look at a full range of possibilities and his capable Nash engineering department was certainly up to the task. Included in the mix of minimum transportation devices were a motorized bicycle, an early forerunner

of the moped, some scooters, a Nash-designed motorcycle whose frame was made up of two stamped steel halves that were then welded together, production motorcycles from several companies, various French, German, Italian and English mini cars, and an extraordinary Nash experimental three wheel car that resembled a motorized rickshaw! This fantastic device, possibly the most astounding Nash experimental car ever, featured two wheels in front and one in the rear. It was powered by a rear mounted 9.9 cubic inch, 5 horsepower Nash engine.

But in the end, none of these vehicles was judged suitable for American tastes. Something that was sized in-between the big Nash Ambassador and the tiny Euroboxes was clearly needed and it was simply a matter of finding the right combination of size, passenger capacity, cost and economy that would appeal to Americans. A combination of European space efficiency and American-sized interior room might do the trick. After much experimentation, the Nash people settled on a reasonable compromise, a compact car on a 100 inch wheelbase. That car was dubbed the Rambler.

George Mason, with cigar, talks to four unidentified men, believed to be members of the press, about a small motorcycle tested by Nash as part of its investigation into the "minimum transportation" field.

As part of their research they also considered even smaller designs, most importantly one that was offered by someone from outside the firm. An independent designer by the name of William Flajole (rhymes with Ma Soul) had designed a car that was small and quite European in flavor. It was a two seater on a short wheelbase and was designed to be a low cost car. Mason evidently was intrigued by its possibilities.

Reportedly, Flajole was contacted first in 1946 by Nash Vice-President Albert M. Wibel, who had formerly been a Ford executive. They met to discuss Flajole's small car ideas. Then in 1948, George Mason and Chief Engineer Meade Moore asked Flajole to submit sketches of his small car design. Although Flajole had considered using a conventional chassis frame design, Nash wanted a car with unit body construction, a Nash feature of considerable importance.

Although some earlier sketches depicted a rear engine/rear drive chassis, the secretive Nash project was to use a conventional front engine/rear drive design.

One concern with Flajole's small car design was its size. It was tiny, at least in comparison with the leviathans then springing forth from most American firms. Mason didn't view the size as a real problem but realized it could prevent the car from becoming a high volume model. This meant that traditional American production methods might not be cost-effective for this type of car. Regardless, Mason saw an opportunity to sell in an unfilled niche in the market and he was determined to investigate its potential.

Flajole sketched a number of ideas. In late 1948, Mason looked through the various proposals and picked what he felt was the design most likely to succeed. Flajole was instructed to draw the car with en-

Members of the press at NXI Preview in Nash garage. Note engineering's Meade Moore standing behind the three-wheel car. It's probable that some other Nash employees are in the crowd.

B. B. Geyer, left, the head of Nash's advertising agency, and Henry C. Doss, vice-president of Nash Sales, in the experimental Nash three-wheel scooter. Mason realized all the "minimum transportation" designs were too small for American tastes, and opted to develop Bill Flajole's Metropolitan design instead.

Nash executives and members of the press view experimental "opposed six" engine during NXI Preview.

closed wheels, a Nash styling feature, but label the car the "Fiat Traveler" to allay any suspicions of Nash competitors.

A modified Fiat Topolino chassis was used as the foundation for a hand-built prototype, since it was light, cheap and about the right size for test purposes. One of the earliest non-traditional approaches Mason was considering was utilizing European components to reduce his tooling costs. His thoughts originally were to build the car in America but use a foreign-made drivetrain to save money. If the car reached production, Italian automaker Fiat would be a likely source for engines and transmissions, so using a Fiat chassis as the basis was as good a place as any to start.

Originally, Flajole considered using interchangeable body panels. In this plan, the front and rear fenders could be cross-interchangeable, left front fender identical to the right rear, and so on. The hood and rear deck would share stampings with each other, and bumpers would interchange front to rear. This would

greatly simplify the stocking of parts at dealerships and body shops, certainly, but more importantly it would greatly reduce the cost of tooling for the new car. The cost savings, which could run into millions of dollars, would greatly reduce the amortization expense, helping ensure a low price tag for the car.

Not everyone at Nash Styling was thrilled to see an independent designer working on a company program but ruffled feathers were soon smoothed and staff members began working on the project. Nash engineering conducted most of the design work on the unitized structure, since they had more experience with that type of construction.

A metal prototype was built during 1949 in the Flajole-Kehrig shops in Utica, Michigan, across from the old Packard Proving Ground. John Kehrig and Bill Flajole worked directly from a one-quarter scale plaster model that Flajole had created. (At this point, automotive designers still worked primarily with plaster models, rather than the clay models that would become the standard in the fifties.) Final trim and paint,

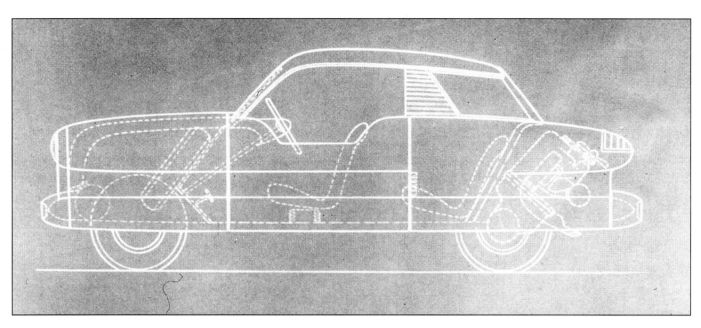

This early sketch by Bill Flajole shows rear-engine concept that was not used in production. Styling is similar to later Pininfarina-built Metropolitan station wagon prototype.

In this sketch, the car is disguised with "Fiat Traveler" name.

however, were done elsewhere, at Meade Moore's insistence. As constructed, the diminutive Nash was a startling sight. Small for that period, it was designed to hold just two passengers. Wheelbase was a mere 84 inches, tread but 40 inches. The whole car weighed just 1,350 pounds. The Fiat Topolino that it was based on was a tiny car that came equipped with an equally tiny engine rated at just 18 horsepower. However, there was sufficient room to fit a larger engine in the Nash prototype, if desired. The car was painted dark maroon and fitted with a white convertible top. Nash dubbed the model "NXI," for Nash Experimental International.

When it came to designing the body, most of the ideas about interchangeable stampings didn't work out. It seems the designers found it possible to come up with interchangeable body stampings or a decent looking car, but not both. However, Flajole was able to design the outer door stampings so they would interchange from side to side, which represented a substantial savings in tooling cost. It was a clever design, helped by a dip in the sheet metal at the window sill,

Two views of Bill Flajole's original NXI plaster model, as it appears today.

1950 NXI prototype was painted deep maroon. Note fully enclosed rear wheel and skirted front wheels. Windshield wipers swept in opposite directions.

where the driver's arm would normally rest. This "arm-rest" design feature (which Flajole called the Pillow Design) helped the little car avoid looking slab-sided.

All four wheels were skirted, the front wheels in a semi-skirt fashion, the rear wheels completely enclosed, which gave the car a lower appearance.

Mason was hoping to keep the price of the car down as low as possible, however, so a few details that were obviously of a cost-saving nature appeared. The bumpers were interchangeable front to rear, thus saving the cost of tooling separate designs. The bumper's center section featured an oval "kissy mouth" shape; when fitted to the front of the vehicle the oval was filled with a conventional toothy grille that bore a family resemblance to other Nash products. At the rear of the car, the bumper's oval was simply left open, with the spare tire stored inside it! The car had no exterior trunk lid, but the luggage compartment could be reached through a door behind the seats. In the interior, the customary glove-box was not included because, Nash claimed, leaving it out saved $5 in costs. The bucket seats and floor shift showed a definite European influence. Perhaps the oddest cost-cutting move were the side windows. These were constructed of plastic and lacked the usual window cranks. Instead, windows were raised

and lowered via a simple (and cheap) strap! According to Nash, conventional wind-up windows might increase the price of the car as much as $25.

Two unique design features of the prototype were the hood, which was flat and rested below the fender line, and the windshield, which dipped at the lower corners. Both features were contrary to industry norms. Although both were described enthusiastically in the press, the hood, which Flajole referred to as the

Bill Flajole's original plaster model, as it appears today. The model has suffered some damage over the years but is still attractive and exciting.

We Talk with Bill Flajole

The man considered the father of the Metropolitan is designer William Flajole. Born in Bay City, Michigan, on February 24, 1915, (although there is some question about the year), Flajole went to work for Chrysler Corporation right out of high school. He later worked for Ford on the first Lincoln Continental. He went on to set up his own independent design company, working as a paid consultant to several companies. It was a fateful day when Nash and Flajole got together to discuss his ideas for a small, lightweight postwar car that evolved into the Metropolitan. We spoke with the great designer in late 1995 about those days:

Q: The original NXI prototype had a Fiat engine in it, didn't it?

Flajole: Oh, I remember that, yes. We built the original car on the smallest Fiat chassis we could find. And it performed very well indeed, but not up to American standards. The American market is rather peculiar in that we like the feeling of weight (in cars) and we like a lot of passengers but we're not willing to pay for it.

Q: Who did you report to at Nash?

Flajole: I reported to the Chief Engineer, who was a fellow named (Meade) Moore. He was not committed to the smaller Nash. I think he saw it realistically in terms of public relations, rather than an engineering problem. Which was easy for him—all you do is get a smaller engine if you want to use less gasoline. But we knew that the public would be very fussy about this small car. We had a lot of puddle jumpers, as we called them, in America, and we had not had a steady market for a small car.

Q: Were you influenced at all by the American Crosley? That was a very small car.

Flajole: I heard about it but I never saw it!

Q: Did you ever deal directly with Nash president George Mason?

Flajole: Yes, he followed all my programs pretty closely. He was a genuine enthusiast of the small car. George really wanted a small car if we could get one. But he realized that the size of the engine was the first consideration.

Q: When you worked on the Met, did you work out of your own studio?

Flajole: In our own institution.

Q: That, I understand, was a firm known as Flajole-Kehrig. Who was Kehrig?

Flajole: John Kehrig was an old fender-bender, as we called it (which means Kehrig was a sheet metal worker who could create prototype bodies from scratch). He had worked at Hudson Motor Car Company in the development section for years, ever since he was a small boy. He worked for Frank Spring. Spring was quite a sensational guy—with his amphibious airplane, his water craft, he was a pretty flamboyant character.

Q: I understand that one of the original concepts for the Metropolitan was that it might have interchangeable body parts where, say, the left rear fender would interchange with the right front fender, to save tooling costs. Do you remember any of that part of the program?

Flajole: Yes, I think in the first part of the program we had that as one of the criteria … we used the whole left side over on the right and the doors were an integral part of that … so we carried the left door over onto the right side of the automobile.

Q: And the bumpers interchanged too, on the NXI prototype?

Flajole: Yes

Q: How did you feel about the final design of the Metropolitan, the one as it appeared to the public—were you pleased with it?

Flajole: Yes.

Q: Overall, how did you enjoy working for Nash?

Flajole: I thought they were wonderful people to deal with. They were unusual in the automobile industry for not having a heavy, assertive attitude. They would tell you what to do and then leave you alone, which I thought was a great arrangement.

William J. Flajole, father of the Metropolitan.

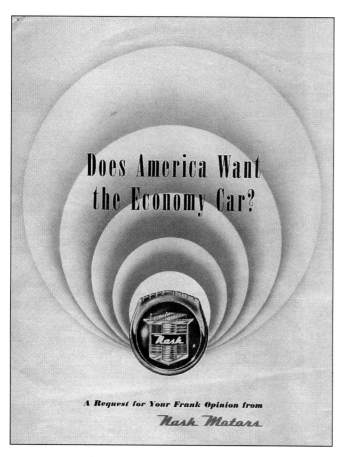

"Drop Hood" (and for which he applied for a patent) received considerably more attention of the two. Both features were later used on production Nash cars.

Thus the NXI. It was a handsome machine, but in many ways it may have been too unconventional. Vehicle size, engine size, seating capacity, interior appointments, everything about it was vastly different from traditional U.S. cars. While it was expected that the new Nash would be unlike any that had come before, it was important that the car not be so unconventional that it wouldn't appeal to a sufficient number of buyers. Mason decided a bit of caution was in order. He was an auto enthusiast of high order, true, but he was also a good businessman. Before launching this new car design onto the market he first needed to make sure it had a reasonable chance of

Auto show handout asked, "Does America want the economy car?"

A big man and a small car. George Walter Mason and the NXI. Mason holds a measuring stick in one hand, a cigar in the other.

George Mason answering questions from the press at an NXI Preview.

selling. Mason hit upon an idea to test the market acceptance of the NXI by doing something no other American auto manufacturer had ever tried before. *He would go out and ask the public if this was the sort of car they wanted!*

This sounds like a rather simple idea in retrospect but at the time it was an unconventional approach to exploring the market for a most unusual car. A series of previews were scheduled for January 1950 at hotels in major cities across the country, beginning with New York on January 4th (at the Waldorf Astoria, no less!) then Washington, D.C. on the 6th, Detroit on the 9th, Chicago on the 11th, Los Angeles on the 18th and San Francisco on the 20th. These were by-invitation-only affairs with a cross section of opinion makers, including the press, appearing on the invitation lists. Nash called these affairs "Surviews," a contraction of Survey-Preview. At each, an NXI prototype was displayed, as well as detailed specifications of the pro-

posed car. Survey questionnaires were handed out to the attendees. These were colorful little pamphlets that carried the heading "Does America Want the Economy Car?" Inside, the booklet exclaimed "There is much of Tomorrow in all Nash does Today" and went on to ask the public for its frank opinion of the car. Being perfectly forthright with the reader, the Nash booklet said of the new car "It has decided advantages—and it has definite limitations." People were invited to "look far down the road with us. Be as critical as you like and let us know what you think."

At each show a Nash spokesperson would demonstrate some of the unusual features of the NXI, such as the unique one piece hood/fender assembly, unusual window arrangement, etc. Mason himself served as spokesman on at least one occasion, but for others he sent his assistant (and soon to become a Nash vice-president) George W. Romney. Romney was a fairly recent addition to Nash management, having joined the company in 1948. One reason he decided to join Nash, rather than rival Packard, which had offered him a better position and more money, was his belief in the future of the small car in America. He had been general manager of the Automobile Manufacturers Association (AMA) when it was headed by George Mason, and he was well acquainted with both Mason and his small car philosophy. Romney was a good speaker, earnest and straightforward, a youthful-looking age 41, handsome and driven by a passion to carry his message to the public. He had once been a salesman for the Aluminum Company of America (ALCOA), back when aluminum was a new, relatively unknown product, and had done well selling it. He enthusiastically showed off the new small car to the public.

What the public saw were specifications of two cars that looked identical but carried different powertrains. Car A, the 18 horsepower version with a four-speed transmission, was meant to be a purely low-priced economy car, capable of a top speed of 60-65 mph but yielding fuel mileage of 45-50 mpg and with a price tag estimated at about $950. Car B carried a 36 horsepower engine and a three-speed transmission, was capable of a 65-70 mph top speed and a

George W. Romney, who vigorously displayed the NXI to the press.

George Mason and two other men show that it was possible to squeeze three passengers into the two-seat NXI.

Man standing at left is believed to be Nash unit-body designer Ted Ulrich, while the man pointing is George Mason's assistant and later head of AMC, George Romney. In the passenger seat is Pinin Farina, with his son-in-law Renzo Carli. Note the signs in the background.

respectable 35-40 mpg, at just $50 higher on the price tag. Both were rather stark but Mason's goal was to sell at or below the $1,000 mark, and the two cars described at the show represented the best way to get there. Also on display were real engines set up on fancy stands, in both the 18 and 36 horsepower versions.

The show car was a two seater, unusual for the time and potentially a problem from a sales point of view. But Nash had strong reasons for settling on that configuration. Some time later, in a paper presented to the American Society of Body Engineers, Chief Mechanical Automotive Engineer W. S. Berry, and Staff Engineer L. H. Nagler wrote:

"Our Management had realized for many years it would be desirable to increase the price coverage of the models produced. Expansion into the high price field was not promising, as the relatively limited mar-

ket was unfavorable to volume sufficient for absorbing the increasingly high tooling costs. Accordingly attention was directed toward lower price vehicles, particularly types of transportation not already produced by American manufacturers."

After studying many types of transportation, including scooters and motorcycles, three-wheel cars, cars with one, two, four, six and eight cylinders, the Nash people had learned a lot about small forms of transportation. To quote Nagler and Berry:

"After reviewing European cars it was considered that certain changes and compromises would have to be made for the American market:

"1. The proposed vehicle must have styling pleasing to the American motorist. The somewhat boxy look of European cars was a result of the necessity of getting four or five passengers in a short wheelbase vehicle.

"2. From this it was reasoned that the proposed vehicle might be proportioned to give adequate room and comfort for the two or three passengers in the front seat; the rear seat, if any, being intended for limited use only. Every attempt was to be made in seat cushion construction and ride to assure adequate comfort for the front seat passengers."

In a nutshell, the new Nash was deliberately designed as a two seater so it could feature flamboyant American styling rather than the cramped, boxy, functional look of postwar European cars. The car would combine the interior spaciousness of a large American car with the fuel efficiency and handling ease of a small European car. The design trade-off was that it would of necessity be a two passenger car.

In a press release dated January 4, 1950, titled "The $1,000 Car?" Nash cautioned the public not to con-

fuse the NXI with an upcoming new Nash car (they were talking about the Rambler) due out within just a few months. In this press release three drivetrains were mentioned for the NXI, 18 and 36 horsepower Fiat engines, both equipped with four-speed manual transmissions, plus a 36 horsepower British "Standard" unit hooked up to a three-speed transmission. The press release noted that other European powerplants could be adapted to the car. Thus, it seems that by this point Mason and Nash had settled on the need to use an imported engine to hold down costs and achieve the low price goal.

Even so, as Mason saw things, that low price wouldn't mean Nash was going after the large-volume "low price" market. He stated, "The NXI is not an attempt by Nash to invade the large volume automobile market. The car, if built, would probably have a rela-

George Mason, right, with unidentified man and the NXI prototype.

tively specialized market potential." That meant, of course, that costs had to be especially low, since he wouldn't have high volume to amortize his investment. Or, it might be that the $1,000 price ceiling would just have to be raised. In either case, it seems Mason was also recognizing a basic truth that eluded so many others who tried to market little cars to Americans—low price, by itself, just wasn't enough. Crosley proved that in the years just prior to World War II and would prove it yet again in the postwar period. An automobile needed more than just a low price tag to sell in large volumes; it also had to be big enough to appeal to families as their primary car. The Nash Rambler was aimed for that market; the Met would aim for the unfilled niche just below it. As Mason put it: "In our judgment, the NXI should meet basic transportation requirements not now served and thus this car should represent 'plus' passenger car sales and would not be competitive with full-size cars now made by Nash or other manufacturers."

Soon, auto show surveys began to be returned to Nash, where the data was totaled up and tabulated. Mason and Romney were encouraged by the initial response. The car was a hit at the Chicago Automobile Show. In Kenosha, Wisconsin, the home of the main Nash factory, 26,000 of the town's 60,000 residents turned out to get a glimpse of it. In all, roughly 236,000 questionnaires were distributed. Thousands were returned to Nash, some with drawings and diagrams attached, some with suggested names for the new car or ideas for improvements to it.

In a later press release, Mason said of the response: "Interest has been unusually strong and sustained. We have received a large number of inquiries,

The NXI on display, probably in Washington, D.C. The man standing at rear of car, cigar in hand, is believed to be Meade Moore of Nash engineering.

many of these from the same individuals who originally expressed interest in the car when we first announced it. In fact, we have received as many as 10 letters from the same individual—written at intervals of two or three months each. We also have received actual orders for the car!"

George Romney had earlier answered some of the letters himself, in his then-capacity of assistant to the president. He wrote to an enthusiastic college student, "We were pleased to receive your letter containing your reaction to our small car idea. We are taking special steps to determine the viewpoint of college students toward this car and expect to obtain the reaction of students at one of our leading colleges in the near future. Certainly, as you say, college students may represent an important market for such a car."

Mason and Nash had done well to ask the public for input, because responses indicated that although the car had solid potential, several important changes would have to be made to help ensure success. Chiefly, the changes centered around the powertrain. The public overwhelmingly voted for the largest engine choice and indicated that the three-speed transmission was preferable. Basically, the public was indicating they wanted better fuel economy than conventional cars but still expected a decent amount of power and were willing to trade off a bit of economy to get it. Inside the car, indications were overwhelmingly clear that buyers wanted a conventional bench seat rather than the narrow buckets shown on the NXI and they wanted a bit more interior room as well. At the time, floor-mounted stickshifts were out of vogue in America. In truth, any family car with a floor

Nash design team 1951: (1-r) Edmund Anderson, director of styling; Bob Thomas, stylist; Royland Taylor, airbrush layouts; Bill Reddig, stylist; Don Butler, accessories.

shifter was looked on as old-fashioned. Thus, it's not surprising the public didn't care for NXI's stickshift and indicated a column shift would be much preferred. The strap-operated plastic side windows were likewise seen as cheap and it was clear they would have to be replaced by conventional winding windows, even if doing so would increase the car's price. Mason began to realize that the original goal of a basic transportation car was going to have to be modified a bit, since it was becoming clear that American drivers didn't care for a bare bones approach. He noted "a widespread general interest in a small, quality, high-style car." But he still held onto the ideal of a low price. "If we build this car," Mr. Mason said, "such changes as the public prefers will be incorporated in the design, within the limits of a $1,000 price tag." The public also asked for more room inside, perhaps a longer wheelbase too, but in this regard Nash had to exhibit restraint. What many prospects were indicating they wanted in early 1950 was a somewhat larger car, and of course the upcoming Rambler would meet their needs perfectly. There was no point in adding so much more room to the NXI that it would end up being a competitor to the Rambler. The purpose of the NXI was to reach for sales below the Rambler's size and price range. Therefore, although the NXI could be made more luxurious inside, it couldn't become too much larger or it might duplicate the Rambler. It had to be aimed at a narrower market niche. Romney and Mason were, however, very much gladdened by the indications that a ready public was out there just waiting for the Ramblers debut.

Mason saw many other virtues in producing the car. "If this car is put into production," he said, "it should contribute to employment both in the United States and in Europe. It would also provide Europe with needed dollar exchange; it would also represent private American enterprise in support of the European assistance program by our government. In doing so, it should also contribute to the effectiveness of the Marshall Plan." These were lofty goals indeed, but George Mason was no small thinker.

The company cautioned the public that it would be a while, if ever, before they could buy such a car from Nash. "These cars are not in production, no tools have been ordered and the cars could not be manu-

Designer Bill Reddig, standing, adds a "highlight line" to a full-size drawing of proposed small Nash. Don Butler, crouching, assists Reddig.

factured for at least one year. It [sic] would be manufactured only if public opinion clearly shows need, desire and willingness to buy them in sufficient quantity," Mason said.

Some time after this, a modified NXI was spotted on the road. Not much was different about it—it was painted a lighter body color and a black convertible top was fitted rather than the white one seen at the Surviews. More substantially changed, however, were the rear wheel openings. This modified NXI had rear wheel wells that were opened up a bit to mimic the look of the front wheels, rather than fully skirted like the original prototype. Also, its gas tank cap rode higher up on the rear fender. On the front fenders, small vent ports, much like Studebaker used, opened to provide fresh air to the interior. The car also appears to have had windshield wipers that swept in parallel motion rather than opposite motion.

After management tallied up the public's response to the NXI Surviews, Nash's small but talented engineering staff, under the aegis of Chief Engineer Meade Moore, began to modify the design so that additional prototypes, incorporating improvements, could be built. Company stylists, under Edmund E. Anderson, worked on a few subtle styling improvements.

Seven months later, on July 12, 1950, Nash reported in a press release that it was nearing completion of production prototypes (versus the less developed styling/concept prototype) although no decision had been made to actually put the car into production. It's known that a series of at least three new prototypes (and possibly as many as six) that included a hardtop model, a revised convertible and a standard coupe type model, were built. The coupe's roof pillars slanted forward, unlike other Nash products, and the rear window didn't wrap around the corners. Changes to the overall design included an increase in wheelbase to 85 inches, increase in horsepower to 42 and a switch to a bench-type front seat. The hood was now separate from the front fenders. The rear wheel wells were opened up slightly and opening vents were added to the front fenders, both features seen earlier on the modified NXI. A bulging chrome scoop was added to the hood, though it most likely was nonfunctional. The styling changes combined to make the car appear slightly longer and more substantial

Clay modeler Charl E. Greene finishes a new clay model reflecting styling changes to the NXI/NKI design. Bill Reddig recalled Greene as "a great guy, very talented."

This side-view drawing, by Nash Styling, shows the evolution of the Met's design. It's believed this is the first time this picture has been published.

looking. These improved cars were called the NKI, for Nash-Kelvinator International, and they can be considered engineering (or production) prototypes, in contrast to the earlier NXI, which was more a concept/show car. The new NKI prototypes were tested extensively. Fuel economy, acceleration, braking, ev-

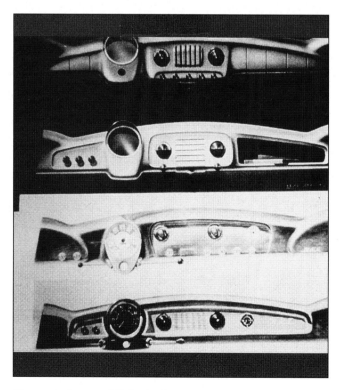

Never before published photo of proposed Met instrument panels, by William Reddig.

erything was scrutinized by Nash with an eye to engineering the design for production. Mason cautioned that it was still uncertain if the tiny auto would ever be offered. "Even if we decide to build the car, we couldn't put it into production any time soon," he said.

"We have been unable to get sufficient steel to meet the demand for our present models. We are expanding our line of Airflyte cars with the new Rambler series. Under these circumstances, we have deferred a final decision on whether to put the NXI into production until we have greater assurance of adequate supply of steel."

The steel supply issue was a real problem. Mason was able to obtain sufficient supplies of steel for Nash car production by paying a premium to steel suppliers but such expense couldn't be borne on a low priced car; not, at least, if a profit was hoped for. This was by no means the only cost pressure beginning to affect the new car program. Tooling costs had shot up after World War II and were still climbing. Labor costs were rising and unions were strong and growing stronger. Inflation, too, was driving up the cost of just about everything, and at this point any other man might have shelved his dreams and forgotten all about a small, inexpensive car. But not George Mason. He had traveled through Europe and was familiar with European expertise in the small car field. Because of the earlier small car testing Nash had done, Mason was familiar with the different overseas automakers, too. Since it was almost a foregone conclusion that an overseas company would be supplying the engines, it was only another small step in the thought process to consider the possibility of finding an experienced partner in Europe to undertake the whole job. Mason began to cast about in Europe for a partner who could supply not only engines, but also assemble the whole car for Nash on a contract basis. If a European maker built the car, costs would be low. Steel supplies wouldn't be an issue either, since the factory would, of course, use European produced steel. With European wages substantially lower than American wages, there was a strong possibility the NKI could be built there, shipped to America and sold for a reasonable price. If it were possible, Mason would do it.

Here, again, George Mason was stepping to the beat of a different drum. The idea of hiring another car company (a foreign one at that) to assemble one's products for sale in America was just about as far out of step with the rest of Detroit as a company could get. This was not merely a different approach; this was almost sacrilege to the stalwarts of the Motor City. Mason evidently didn't feel bound to anyone else's idea of convention, however. If the only way to turn a profit on this size automobile was to make it overseas, then so be it.

Meade Moore of Engineering began looking at plants in various European countries. Finally, a British producer was chosen (most likely helped by the effect of a recently devalued British pound). On October 5, 1952, Nash-Kelvinator released a statement that said, "Negotiations between Nash and two long estab-lished British automotive firms have been completed for the production, during the later part of 1953, of the new car for distribution in the United States and Canada." It was noted that a name had not been settled on for the new car, which the release still referred to as the NXI. George Mason explained the rationale behind his decision to go ahead with the program.

"The overwhelmingly favorable response to the nationwide NXI survey and the basic economic and motoring trends convinced us that there is a market for a compact car of this type. Many of the changes we have incorporated in prototype models resulted from suggestions made by motorists who saw the first experimental car back in early 1950."

Austin Motor Company, Ltd., of Birmingham, England, the largest automobile company outside of the United States, was chosen to produce the finished cars. Fisher & Ludlow, Ltd., a body manufacturer also of Birmingham, was picked to supply the unitized bodies. Austin would build the car to Nash's specifications, although it was expected that the bulk of the chassis and drivetrain parts would be British sourced. Final assembly would take place at Austin's Longbridge plant.

Final specifications now began to be set and Nash Styling started working towards finalizing the appearance of the car. It was decided to endow it with several Nash styling marks so the public could readily identify it as a Nash product. After all, the Nash name

This is believed to be a late prototype. The car appears nearly identical to the production version, but a close look reveals it has a one-piece rear window instead of the three-piece type used in production. Note the "Custom" nameplate on the left front fender and full-dish wheel covers, both unique features. Background appears to be the Nash styling studios.

was well respected, and a foreign car that was backed by Nash's strong dealer network would be seen as having a considerable advantage over other imported cars.

The basic look mimicked the 1952-1954 Nash Statesman, with notched armrests on the door outer skins, skirted (enclosed) wheels, and a windshield with dropped lower edges. The "kissy-mouth" grille was replaced by a higher mounted oval with inset floating bar that was a near copy of the 1953-1954 Rambler. The placement of the front bumper guards and turn signal lights were both nearly identical to the Rambler. The fender side vent doors were gone, replaced by a neat looking raised air inlet, just forward of the windshield like other Nashes. Conventional bumpers were fitted front and back. Also at the rear, the open section where the spare tire once slid in was eliminated entirely. The spare tire was now carried upright in a rear-mounted continental style carrier. There was no trunk lid at all but the rear storage area could be reached from inside the car via an access door in the rear parcel area.

The Nash designers worked a minor miracle. The NKI (née NXI) was now instantly recognizable as a product of Nash Motors and bore a family resemblance to the rest of the line. Now it was up to Nash Engineering to ensure the product would live up to the Nash heritage of dependable motoring, and to Nash Sales to convince its dealer organization to adopt this foreigner as one of its own. That could prove to be a tough sell. The Crosley automobile, a Lilliput of a car made in Indiana, was nearing the end of its production, a victim of customer disinterest in small cars. Even Volkswagen would sell less than 1,000 cars in the United States for 1952.

The small car was an odd duck in America at that time. They appealed to an offbeat crowd, avantgarde, far out of the mainstream. Small cars wouldn't become a success unless they somehow could be made palatable to a larger segment of the buying public. It was up to Mason and company to use their skills to make Americans suddenly want something that they hadn't seemed to want before. Looking back, we can realize that this was a difficult task for any company to attempt, let alone a small independent such as Nash. Nash management wasn't staffed with fainthearted men, however. Far from it—both Mason and Romney were eager for the challenge. The time had come to put up or shut up and for George Mason, there was only one choice.

Chapter Two

From Longbridge With Love (1954-1955)

With the decision to put the baby Nash into full scale production came several new challenges. The car would need further engineering, suppliers had to be contracted with for the hundreds of parts needed to make the NKI, and marketing plans had to be drawn up. Also, an advertising program that could overcome American indifference toward small cars had to be developed, dealers had to be trained in servicing and selling a new type of car and even Nash's own corporate sales organization, headed by Henry Clay Doss, would need to be convinced that the new product would enhance rather than detract from Nash's image in the market. Some Nash executives openly belittled the car as a "puddle jumper" and tried to convince Mason to scuttle his plans to build

it. They could have saved their breath. Mason held onto his vision of the future and he was not likely to sway from that dedication. He believed Nash needed to be an innovative company in order to survive and prosper, and the NKI obviously was an innovative product. Let others trade with the carriage set, Mason felt; he would look for opportunities in the lower-price market categories. A few Nash executives also approached George Romney with a plea to talk Mason out of producing the car but unfortunately for them, Romney was firmly behind Mason's small car plans.

But it would be a while before the car could be introduced. An October 5, 1952, press release gave a hint at the interval that could be expected. A date for

Early press photo clearly shows "NKI Custom" badging on front fender. Note that hubcaps are unbranded, but Nash grille badge is present.

This may be an early pre-production prototype. Look closely and you can see the front fender is dented. It's felt that if Nash had a ready supply of production cars it wouldn't have used this obviously damaged car for photography—thus it's probably an early pre-production car.

the public introduction of the car had not been fixed, according to the news release, but "it will not be available for sale before the latter part of next year." That seemed to indicate late 1953, which meant it would have to debut as a 1954 model. Fair enough.

The question of who the parts and components suppliers would be was answered quite handily: they would nearly all be British. Quoting again from the A.S.B.E. paper of W. S. Berry and L. H. Nagler: "To minimize the skyrocketing costs of tooling and engineering development in this country since World War II, it was decided to build initially as many components as possible abroad. In fact, the basic thesis of the NXI involved taking advantage of a favorable foreign exchange and the lower cost of engineering and tooling available in many European countries.... The final powerplant selected was one of Austin's regular production units, and one that had proved itself in large numbers of Austin cars."

Actually, as things worked out, all parts of the NKI would be supplied by English firms, with the sole exception of the headlamps. The reason for that exception, according to Nagler and Berry, was simply that

"English lights do not meet American legal and technical requirements."

Tires were British Goodyear, all natural rubber, and electrical components were from the firm of Lucas—later to become infamously nicknamed the "Prince of Darkness." Instruments were Smiths, another well-known British firm that, oddly enough, also supplied the jack. The engine, as noted, was a standard production Austin unit, an overhead valve, inline four-cylinder. It was what Austin termed its A-40 series engine, 1200cc, developing 42 horsepower. Transmission choices were limited: three-speed manual was all there was. This gearbox, also from Austin, was an A-40 series, normally a four-speed, but in this application had first gear removed in recognition of America's preference for three-speed transmissions. The gear shifter itself was mounted on the dash just below and offset from the steering wheel, a setup nearly identical to the Rambler's.

The handbrake was operated by a pull lever that sprouted from the floor just to the left of the driver's knees. This setup would later be the focus of complaints from some automotive testers who considered it an inconvenient and old-fashioned layout, but it worked well enough regardless. Along the same lines, though not quite so anachronistic, was the manual choke operated by a pull knob on the dash. Automatic chokes were common enough back then, but were not yet in universal use, especially among low priced cars. The large diameter steering wheel had good heft and a solid feel for easy steering effort. Brakes were Girling hydraulics, not, as some silly road tester later reported, cable actuated mechanical brakes.

These were all first-class components—no second rate or sub-par items to be found. Nash had always enjoyed a reputation for building solid, reliable machines, cars that anyone could be proud to own. The Nash brand, aside from the Rambler, was firmly established in the public's mind as a medium and higher price car, an automobile for the upper reaches of the middle class. Mason wouldn't allow that fine reputation to be sullied by substandard service or mediocre performance. The littlest Nash would be built properly or not at all.

Austin's Longbridge factory was a good one. It soon began to assemble production prototypes to test its tooling and processes and also to provide more test cars for Nash to study. By this point, 1953, it had been decided to retain the NKI name on the little car when it entered production. The name was nearly identical to that of the NXI prototype car that so many auto show visitors around the country had viewed, so it had already built up a certain amount of name recognition in the market. It was a good name, too, since the initials clearly represented what the car was: an international joint venture product from Nash-Kelvinator. Mason had talked about using the new car to help increase international sales, and that idea could likewise be said to be symbolized in the nameplate. So going with the NKI name was an easy decision for Nash.

Nash's Airflyte unitized construction was going to be one of the biggest selling features of the new car, of course. Operating economy, fuel economy and low purchase price were all salient features but it would be beneficial to Nash if those qualities were justified and reinforced in the consumer's mind by first addressing a very real fear that many Americans had about small cars: *were they unsafe?*

Early press photo of convertible still has NKI Custom badge.

Met hardtop transports mother and daughter to the music school, circa 1954. Note unbranded hubcaps.

As long as small cars utilized a conventional frame design with bolted-on body, exactly like most big cars of the day, anybody could figure out that they would be less safe in a crash than in a large car, since when two identical designs collide the margin of safety usually goes to whichever is packing the greater amount of weight. But Nash, with its advanced unitized body/ frame structure, was viewed by the public as having discovered a way to build stronger, safer cars whose crash-worthiness relied on structural design integrity rather than raw mass. Thus the NKI wouldn't necessarily suffer the suspicions of the "safety question" that plagued other small imports.

Nash NKI buyers wouldn't have to worry about another problem that import owners faced in the 1950s (and 1960s for that matter): where to obtain replacement parts and service? The NKI would have the backing of Nash's solid and dependable dealer force, or at least the greater percentage of them. A few Nash dealers opted not to stock or sell the NKI, a decision they probably regretted in later years.

By 1953, Nash-Kelvinator had been in the automobile business for over fifty years and the grand old company was staffed by some of the ablest automobile men in the industry. The myriad problems of engineering, parts stocking, service training, advertising planning, sales promotion and all the rest were worked through in a deliberate, careful and competent manner. Nash was that sort of company—prudent and capable.

Early model still carries "NKI Custom" nameplate, before the switch to "Metropolitan" name.

By fall, the pieces had all come together. The Austin assembly line began building regular production cars in October of 1953. That would ordinarily be considered a late month to start production, since it generally takes some time to work a new assembly line up to regular production speed, and then it takes many weeks for a new automobile to fill the pipeline from the factory to the shipping areas to the dealerships and to build an adequate inventory of cars for announcement day. All it meant, simply, was that the new car couldn't be formally introduced to the public until the spring of 1954. The serial numbers for the production models began with 1001 and those first cars coming off the line carried the nameplate "NKI Custom" on the right front fender.

Because of the long supply line, running from England to the USA and then extending out to the forty-eight states, it was decided that the list of color choices and options had to be kept to a minimum, since shoppers wouldn't be able to custom order an NKI. Buyers could either purchase from dealer stock or have the dealer locate a car for them from zone inventory, and therefore the fewer choices offered would mean the greater likelihood that a car with the right color and equipment could be found in stock. Only four colors were offered at first: Spruce Green, Canyon Red, Caribbean Blue and Croton Green. Hardtops all came with the roof painted a contrasting Mist Gray. Convertible top color was tan if the car was Spruce Green, black if the car was Croton Green or Canyon Red, while either tan or black tops could be had on convertibles painted Caribbean Blue.

As was customary, Nash engineers decided to road test a few early production cars for quality and performance. The job fell to a team led by a young engineer named Carl Chakmakian, who thought up an idea to provide the company with increased value from the testing. Chakmakian decided to test two new NKIs on a closed track, one car for economy and one for endurance. His plan was to run the cars around the clock, racking up many miles and much experience from the testing, while at the same time recording the tests on movie film that could later be used to show the dealers (and possibly the public) how well the car performed. In an Interdepartmental Letter written afterwards, Chakmakian explained his idea thusly:

"Today, more than ever, a new automobile such as the NKI must be a proven performer before a manufacturer dares to subject it to the public's critical eye. However, the proof must be more convincing than the evidence that is recorded in engineering departments or the claims appearing in advertising copy—the prospective buyer must be shown that the car will live up to its laboratory reputation on the open road. The primary objective of the test was to dramatically validate the performance, fuel economy, and endurance of the 1954 NKI. To this end, it was planned to conduct two distinct types of performance runs simultaneously dur-

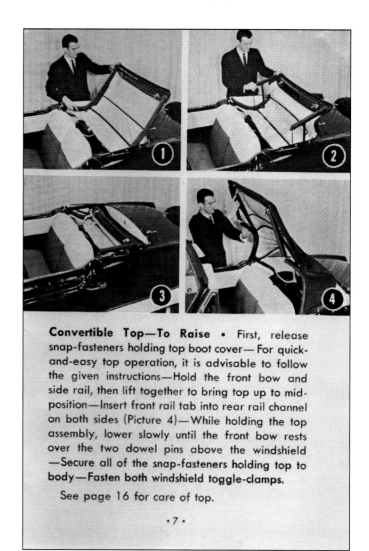

Convertible Top—To Raise • First, release snap-fasteners holding top boot cover—For quick-and-easy top operation, it is advisable to follow the given instructions—Hold the front bow and side rail, then lift together to bring top up to mid-position—Insert front rail tab into rear rail channel on both sides (Picture 4)—While holding the top assembly, lower slowly until the front bow rests over the two dowel pins above the windshield —Secure all of the snap-fasteners holding top to body—Fasten both windshield toggle-clamps.

See page 16 for care of top.

• 7 •

Nash/AMC Engineer Carl Chakmakian appeared in the Metropolitan owner's manual, demonstrating operation of convertible top.

ing the 24-hour period. One car was to demonstrate exceptional fuel economy with endurance, while the other NKI demonstrated speed with endurance—both establishing the overall excellence of the NKI design and the reliability of its component parts."

Chakmakian settled on a new NASCAR race track at Raleigh, North Carolina, after first ruling out both the Bonneville Salt Flats, because surface water reportedly was present there, and the Indianapolis Speedway, which had construction work going on.

The two NKI Customs chosen were stock, both early production models. The endurance car was serial number E-1008, indicating it was the eighth production car built. The fuel economy car's serial number of E-1013 indicates it was the thirteenth car off the assembly line. Evidently, Chakmakian didn't feel thirteen was an unlucky number to choose!

Nash Research Department technicians and mechanics performed the preparation work on the two

We Talk with Carl Chakmakian!

Q: What was your occupation at Nash? Were you a test driver?

CHAKMAKIAN: I'm a graduate engineer. I started working (for Nash) in March of 1953 in the engineering product planning group. I seemed to have an affinity for cars and they asked me to do it [to test drive the new Mets]. We took three or four of them down to the Raleigh Speedway. Had a hell of a good time.

Q: What did you think the first time you saw the car?

CHAKMAKIAN: Well, my first reaction was it wasn't too good looking; I was not involved in the design of it at all. The running gear wasn't bad, you know the engine and that stuff....

Q: Did you think it was too small?

CHAKMAKIAN: No, I thought it was okay for size. One thing I think I was responsible for pushing was, after a few years they decided to put a trunk lid on it, which they didn't have on the first ones....

Q: How many different Metropolitans did you test drive during that testing period?

CHAKMAKIAN: There was myself and three other guys.... I think it was a total of four vehicles. And oddly enough we had no trouble with them; we drove them down there, ran 'em around the track for a couple days and drove 'em back.

Q: They tested out okay?

CHAKMAKIAN: They tested out fine. Had no mechanical troubles, which is really quite unusual...for any sort of a car.

Q: Did you buy one?

CHAKMAKIAN: No, I fell in love with a Nash-Healey and I bought one. In fact, I've still got it...it's in super shape!

production NKI Customs. The cars were not altered or modified, since the aim of the tests was to prove the capabilities of the car as it came from the factory. Both cars were then driven the 800 mile distance to the track (with no mechanical troubles reported, by the way), arriving at the track on the evening of December 2, 1953, several days in advance of the scheduled testing.

Chakmakian and his crew used the time to go over the procedures they would use for changing drivers on the go, for fuel fill ups, etc. Several practice runs were also made at this time, both to try out procedures and to fine tune the program. The Nash team's confidence grew as test time neared, undaunted by a few smart aleck remarks made by some of the NASCAR personnel. Perhaps those doubters should be forgiven; after all, what other reaction could be expected when southern stock car enthusiasts came face-to-face for the first time with a teeny-weenie Nash?

Test Day arrived as scheduled, December 7th, though the start of the testing was delayed a couple of hours beyond the noon target. Regardless, Chakmakian and team were raring to go. The fuel economy test was to be a nonstop 24-hour marathon, with driver changes, performed on the run, every three hours to avoid over-tiring the men. Changing drivers required the car to be slowed down to a fast walk, as one driver hopped out the passenger door and the new driver clambered in through the driver's side door. Gasoline, too, was added while the car was in motion, via a special gas tank filler attached to the side of the car.

The endurance car was also run for twenty-four hours; however, it was allowed to pit for tire changes every two to three hours, since the track's highly abrasive asphalt aggregate surface, combined with the high speeds the little car was being driven, caused rapid tire wear. However, each time the car was pitted, NASCAR timers would stop the clock to ensure a true twenty-four-hour run.

The drivers slept in parked cars between runs. The pit crews serviced and gassed the autos at regular intervals, fighting the cold temperatures by warming themselves over an oil drum filled with burning rubbish. These were certainly not deluxe accommodations, but on the whole it must have been great fun nonetheless.

In the midst of this highly secretive testing, who should suddenly appear but one of America's most famous and beloved automobile writers, Tom McCahill of *Mechanix Illustrated* fame. "Uncle" Tom had been alerted by NASCAR's Bill France that tests of the secret, still-unannounced, baby Nash were being held at one of his tracks. McCahill, a longtime admirer of Nash products, couldn't resist the chance to be the first auto tester in America to see the new car. He did more than just view it, though. The Nash people let him test drive a spare NKI, both on and off the track.

McCahill later reported that the NKI "is a nice-handling car with plenty of control and amazing dig." A big man who liked fast cars, McCahill still came away with a favorable impression of the little machine. "If you are the owner of a big Detroit battleship," he wrote, "and are thinking about an extra car or a third jalopy for Junior, this would be a hard rig to beat for quick loops around the neighborhood." After admitting he had come predisposed to scorn the small car, McCahill confessed that the NKI "...is much better than I anticipated. In fact, I like it."

The economy car finished at 2 p.m. the following day, the endurance car 2-1/2 hours later, due to the accumulated pit stops. The economy car achieved 41.57 mpg, while the endurance car had managed an average speed of 61.24 mph, both excellent records. Proof of the overall quality of the new car could be found in the fact that neither NKI had required any repairs or adjustments. Mason and company had done a special thing indeed; they had produced a quality small car for Americans. Now all they had to do was sell it.

A change was soon decided on for the NKI Custom, a major change that required little tooling but a bit of scrambling for Nash to accomplish in time. It was felt that, while the NKI name was a good one it was not quite good enough. Several new names were discussed, finally boiling down to a short list of choices that included: "Cadet," "Scot," "Commuter," "Nike"(!) and "Runabout."

But in the end a new name was picked that seemed more representative of the product than even NKI was. After all, this was not an all-purpose family sedan nor a big travel barge. This was a small automobile for the urban dweller or for the commuter. It was meant to be a housewive's shopping car, or a girl's best friend, not a cruiser built for the endless roadways of the Great Plains. Quite the contrary; this car was for the suburbs and the metropolis. So it was decided to call it the Metropolitan.

Metropolitan. A very good name indeed, both classy and cute. It summoned forth visions of swank city life, adventure-filled days in New York, perhaps, with trips to the opera, shopping excursions on Fifth

Television actor John Bromfield with his Met convertible.

Avenue, the view from atop the Empire State Building and the glamour of the Great White Way, all that is stylish and fun and exciting. Metropolitan. From the palm-lined freeways of Los Angeles to the hot sandy beach at Daytona, to the brisk coastal beauty of Seattle and the tidy boardwalk of Atlantic City, and every city and college town in between, America would come to know and love the Metropolitan.

One potential problem was that the International Harvester company held the rights to the name Metro, which it used for a line of walk-in vans it manufactured in Bridgeport, Connecticut. AMC worked it out with IH, which insisted that the Met never be referred to in print as a "Metro," but instead be known by its full name—Metropolitan.

It was especially easy for Nash to choose that name since the company had used it many years earlier on a 1912 Rambler touring car. Bill Flajole maintains that he had dubbed his concept a "Metropolitan" while it was still just a sketch. The name change was so precipitate, however, that early production cars went out the door carrying NKI nameplates, and dozens of early press photos had been printed that showed the car wearing the NKI badge. Nash responded by changing the nameplates of cars in stock, where possible, and altering subsequent press photos so that they would now show the

Metropolitan name. To simplify the changeover as much as possible, the new "Metropolitan" nameplate was designed to utilize the same fender holes that had held the NKI Custom script. According to internal company memos, the production line continued drilling the same fender holes as before, but, lacking a nameplate to install, simply shipped the cars without badges. Something over 3,000 Metropolitan nameplates had to be air-shipped to the United States for installation on in-stock cars in time for announcement day. Further proof of how abrupt the timing of the name change was can be seen by the date on Chakmakian's Interdepartmental Letter, December 16, 1953, wherein he repeatedly refers to the car as the NKI. Company documents prove the new name was still under consideration even as late as mid-January of its introductory year. According to Nash-Kelvinator internal memos, the Metropolitan name was officially adopted effective January 22, 1954, less than two months before the new car's official announcement day. That was close timing indeed.

Selling the new car would be the responsibility of the Nash sales organization, a group both proud and professional although perhaps a bit complacent after too many years of easy "selling" during the postwar sellers market. Complacency was a problem that had affected every company in the auto business, but the

A Metropolitan sales meeting March 11, 1954, includes: (l-r) George W. Mason, CEO Nash-Kelvinator; George W. Romney, executive vice-president; Henry Clay Doss, vice-president sales; James Watson, Nash general sales manager; Mr. Thompson, Nash Detroit zone manager.

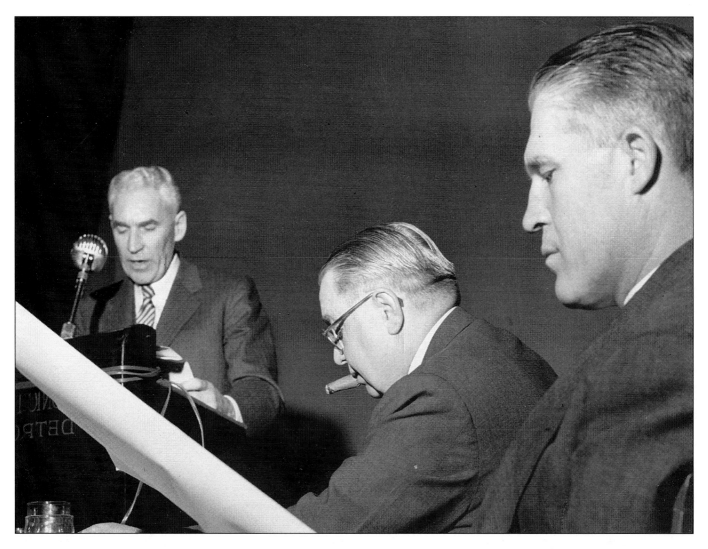

James Watson delivers a speech about the new Metropolitan, while his bosses George W. Mason (with customary cigar) and George W. Romney, listen, during Detroit meeting on March 11, 1954.

Metropolitans on a Stick?

Most people are familiar with that favorite summer barbecue treat called shish kabobs, right? Chunks of meat and vegetables skewered on metal rods, slowly rotating over a fire. Yummy, right?

Picture this scene at the Austin plant in 1954: Metropolitan bodies, rotating slowly, skewered on metal rods.

How's that, you say?

According to the ASBE paper co-authored by L.H. Nagler and W.S. Berry, that's exactly what occurred during one phase of painting Metropolitan bodies. To quote from the paper:

"If the Continental tire mounting were to be removed it would reveal a hole which lines up with a hole in the dash provided for the car heater. . . . A long bar, about four inches in diameter, is inserted through these holes in the body to carry the unpainted body through the priming dip. The entire body assembly is rotated on this bar as it is submerged in the primer. This assures that priming paint coats even the inside of the box section."

bitter Chevy-Ford sales war that had begun the prior year was starting to wake up executives to the need to improve sales skills throughout their organizations.

Nash had another, larger problem. Henry Clay Doss, Nash vice-president in charge of sales, was a confirmed big car man and was rather lukewarm about small cars. For the long term, Mason and Romney knew they would need to cast around for a new man to replace Doss, one who would be more dedicated in efforts to selling Ramblers and Metropolitans. For the near term, though, just one step down on the organization chart was a good man, James W. Watson, who truly liked small cars. He was going to give the Metropolitan a good send-off no matter what.

Jim Watson, age 53 at the time, had spent most of his career in auto sales, working at several companies until finally settling at Nash in 1945. He'd held mostly lower level zone sales positions until his most recent promotion, in February of 1954, to general sales manager for Nash Motors Division, just one month away from the Metropolitan's big announcement date.

It appears that cars were already arriving at dealerships at a steady pace. Dealers apparently were selling them too, although the big push would come in March when the whole country would learn about the new car. Things were done differently in those days, and a new car announcement was a real show. Nash, as one of the oldest mass producers in America, knew how to do it right.

A lot of detail work went into making sure the word got out that a whole new kind of car was coming to America. First came the announcement show for dealers, and then a press introduction. Finally, there came the big roll-out for the public, held at Nash dealerships throughout America on March 19, 1954, with customers and potential buyers invited in to see a car that was both genuinely new and intriguingly different.

Catalog announces "The Exciting New Metropolitan."

Miss America 1954, Evelyn Ay, unveils the exciting new Metropolitan.

Since this was a car that would be aimed at both male and female drivers, it made sense to provide advertising and press photos that showed both males and females actually driving the cars, rather than relegating women to their usual passive role as passengers. The first Metropolitan sales catalog used that balanced approach; both men and women were pictured at the wheel. The cover of the first Met catalog is quite attractive, a nighttime sky filled with a bursting fireworks display and a handsome headline that announces, in script, **"THE EXCITING NEW METRO-POLITAN."**

The catalog, a bit surprisingly, refers to the Met as a "he-man car, a car that hustles up steepest hills, over roughest roads, and rides with unbelievable smoothness."

While the pitch was going to be aimed at both women and "he-men," it was traditional in those days to use pretty girls to help introduce a new car. That being the case, why not go all out to promote the new car? Why not have the most beautiful girl in America help show off this new car to the public? **WHY NOT HAVE MISS AMERICA SHOWCASE THE MET?**

Nash was a proud sponsor of the Miss America pageant. Even when its business was suffering an off-year such as 1954, Nash continued its support. That was a most welcome circumstance since it meant that the year's winner, the lovely Miss Evelyn Ay of Pennsylvania, could help announce the new Metropolitan to the public. Miss Ay didn't need to buy a car herself though; Nash provided her family a new Ambassador. But she was so taken by the beauty of the Met that she used her own money to buy a new Metropolitan as a gift to her brother! Nice girl, that Evelyn Ay, very nice indeed.

Nash General Sales Manager Jim Watson, in a 25 page printed handout titled "WHAT THE METROPOLITAN MEANS TO THE NASH DEALER, SALESMAN, AND OWNER," dated May 1954, wrote *"The introduction of the Metropolitan adds a milestone to the progress of Nash dealers and salesmen. This could be the beginning of a revolution in the thinking of the American people regarding the automobile. This METROPOLITAN may make many men realize they don't need the Queen Mary to cross the Delaware. It may cause women to realize they don't need to shop for hairpins in a two ton car."* Sexist comment aside, Watson was right on. As he further stated, *"Here is a car the entire country will be discussing,"* suggesting that the new car would thus *" ...stimulate floor traffic and enable Nash dealers to meet many people who may have never before considered visiting their salesrooms."* Watson saw many pos-

Evelyn Ay, Miss America 1954.

We Talk with Miss America!

Evelyn Ay Sempier, Miss America 1954, was kind enough to grant us an interview and to recall for our readers the excitement of both the Nash Metropolitan introduction and Nash Motors itself. Evelyn can be considered the original "Metropolitan Girl" because she was the first Miss America to show off the car. As she recalls, "I was Miss America in 1954 and that was the year that the Metropolitan was introduced. I thought it was exciting and the first thing I did was buy one for my brother." We asked her to tell us more about that. Why did she buy one for her brother? "We came from a middle class family and he was always into cars and I thought 'oh wow' what can I do for my brother, in the serendipity of being Miss America? And I bought him one." She purchased it from the local Nash dealer in Ephrata, Pennsylvania.

"I thought it was a great fun car…and I would like to say that the relationship (with Nash Motors) was one of the finest relationships…and I've had a lot of commercial relationships in the

40 years since…it was one of the finest, genuine relationships I ever had. I, as a Miss America, was always treated very genuinely, I was not a 'product.'"

Evelyn explained for us some of the ways Nash sponsored her: "What allowed me to see much of America was because of Nash…if a community had a celebration and they could not afford the small price, at that time, of bringing Miss America, Nash would say, "I will bring Miss America to your community," and they would pay (the fee) to bring me to that community. They (Nash) were most generous in sponsoring Miss America in many parts of America."

Evelyn didn't buy a Met of her own, though. As Miss America, her family got the flagship of the Nash line, a flashy new Ambassador. She remembers that car fondly, too. "That wonderful Nash Ambassador! It was red and white and the seat went down, oh, it was marvelous!"

Owner's manual for 1954 Metropolitan.

sibilities for the new car. *"Here is the opportunity for a Nash dealer to sell a METROPOLITAN to owners of two, three or even four cars. Here is the opportunity to sell those people who often want to have the first of everything new, and those who take pride in having cars different from most people. Here is also the opportunity to sell the Ambassador, Statesman, or Rambler to people interested in seeing the METROPOLITAN, but whose purchase may not be suitable for their needs."*

Watson explained where the buyers might come from. *"The Census Bureau forecasts,"* he wrote, *"that an additional 500,000 families will buy a second car for the first time in 1954."* To allay fears that the Met might be too underpowered for American roads, Watson stressed, *"From the Ambassador down to the METROPOLITAN, [Nash cars] have sufficient power for any and all normal or legal driving requirements. There is not a single car in the line which cannot land a person in jail if its full power and speed is used at the wrong time, in the wrong places."*

As Watson noted in several charts, Nash, with a total of five wheelbases ranging from the 85 inch Met to

the 121-1/4 inch Ambassador, now offered more choices than any other franchise. He wrote: *"Nash dealers with a greater selection of new cars available than any other franchised automobile dealer represents a one-stop store for the motor car buyer. Prospects actually do not need to go any place else to get the type, or types of cars that best suit their needs."* He urged Nash dealers to do *" ...the best job of selling and servicing of owners cars that it is possible for them to do.... Here's a new chance to prove your selling strength. Good luck to all of you."*

Really, though, not a lot of luck was going to be needed. Mason, realizing the Metropolitan was a unique product and it would take time for the public to fully accept it, set a modest sales goal for the tiny car. And at any rate, the Met was a pretty unusual car for the time and the public soon swarmed into showrooms just to get a look at it.

What they saw when they got there was a machine that was exactly what it looked like: Bill Flajole's NXI design, updated and improved in areas the public had indicated needed improvement, and yet still close to its original concept in size and utility. It boasted Nash Airflyte unitized construction for safety and wore chrome "Airflyte" script on its dashboard's centrally mounted ashtray. Two body styles were available, hardtop and convertible. Interestingly, the Met convertible didn't require extra bracing in the floor area nor did it have to resort to the overhead rails used on the Rambler convertible. Nash explained that the strong construction of the body, combined with the short wheelbase, provided sufficient rigidity so that side rails weren't necessary. In reality, the convertible had been designed and engineered first, with all the necessary strengthening members built in. The coupe evolved later, thus benefiting from the extra strong design.

The wheelbase was 85 inches and overall length came in at 149-1/2 inches. Width was 61-1/2 inches,

The family of John A. Conde, assistant director of public relations at AMC, in Mrs. Conde's Metropolitan.

"Another Smash Hit from Nash," according to this Nash advertisement.

generous enough for two adults but a bit snug for three. This was an important point to realize since the rear seat area was absolutely tiny. Nash explained the interior features in a Model Information File it issued December 14, 1953. "Although the [Metropolitan] is listed as a three-passenger car in the A.M.A. Specifications, the seating of three adults of normal size in the front seat results in a squeeze that eventually becomes quite uncomfortable. The front seat offers excellent accommodations for two passengers. Thus, the advertising copy and art should not positively state that three passengers can ride in comfort in the front seat. The rear seat is primarily a utility seat for small children, and also functions as a bench for packages." The artwork in the brochure reflected this edict, with only one or two adults shown in the front and only children in the rear area. Nash thus dealt with the issue honestly and didn't try to make the Met seem like more than it was.

There were just two models offered, the 541 Convertible and the 542 Hardtop, the latter of which Nash, following industry practice, referred to as a "Hardtop Convertible."

Interior trim came in only one level: Custom! Some of the lessons learned from the successful introduction of the Rambler, in 1950, were carried over to the

Met. Like the Rambler, Mets came with much more standard equipment than a buyer would normally expect. The seat was upholstered in genuine leather and beige Nylon-face Bedford Cord, which Nash proudly noted was exactly the same as the standard trim in the top line Ambassador and Statesman Country Club models. A continental spare tire was standard, as were directional turn signals, electric windshield wipers, ashtray, cigarette lighter, dual sun visors, two-tone paint (on hardtop models) and foam rubber front seat cushion.

As noted earlier, the engine was the OHV Austin A-40 four-cylinder, a capable mill that generated 42 horsepower. Nash Engineering had specified that it be fitted with four piston rings, rather than the usual three, an important improvement. An oil bath air cleaner was standard. Tires, although they appeared rather small, were 5.20x13, four-ply blackwall, with whitewalls available at extra cost. Nash's famed Weather Eye heating system was also available, as was an optional radio and optional partial flow oil filter. (It was quite common in the fifties for oil filters to be optional!) Automatic transmission and air conditioning were not available at all. In fact, these never would be offered on Metropolitans. Such things were fairly new to the market back then and were some-

Factory press photo of Metropolitan hardtop (top) shows its amazing resemblance to the 1953-54 Nash Rambler (bottom).

Handsome Met and happy owner—a 1954 Nash Metropolitan hardtop. Note "Nash" brand on hubcaps.

From the 1954 Metropolitan data book, Met interior was nicely trimmed, roomy for two.

It is not known for certain but is possible that this Met, fitted with a trunk rack and leather hold-down straps, belonged to Meade Moore of Nash engineering.

what rare even on big, expensive cars. It was felt that few buyers would want them on a low-priced car such as the Metropolitan.

A 12-volt electrical system was used, rather than the six-volt systems then fitted to many U.S. cars. The front suspension was entirely English manufactured, but was based on the "Airflex" design Nash used on all its cars. Coil springs were mounted high up and angled in a manner that Nash likened to sea-legs. Rear suspension was conventional leaf springs.

Other Nash products of the era wore the crest of Farina, famed Italian stylist, but not the Metropolitan. The reason was simple: Pinin Farina had nothing to do with styling the car. Nash Styling was given the credit for the job although, of course, that included Bill Flajole, since he was under contract to Nash. But the Met did carry a great deal of family resemblance with the bigger Nash cars, so Farina's influence seemed readily apparent even though he hadn't actually worked on the Met. Nash advised its advertising executives that the Met " ...may be advertised as hav-

ing Pinin Farina continental styling, but Farina should not be credited with the actual job." In retrospect, one could argue that the Met's styling influenced the look of Nash's big cars!

All the pieces were now in place. The Metropolitan officially went on sale to the public on March 19, 1954, fully researched, well engineered, quality built and having sufficient inventory in dealers' hands, with lovely Miss America helping to introduce it, and with public excitement at a high pitch. The first thing just about everybody wanted to know was: "HOW MUCH DOES IT COST?" They weren't disappointed. Early rumors had speculated the price might be "between $1,600 and $1,700," which would have had the Met competing with the bottom line Rambler models. Luckily, Nash figured that out and realized the Met would have to come in lower if it hoped to attract shoppers. Prices were set at just $1,469 for the convertible, $1,445 for the hardtop. That was fairly cheap money, even back then, being just slightly more expensive than a stripped Henry J, which, although

Advertisement from Women's Wear Daily, Thursday, July 1, 1954, shows well-dressed woman and her Met.

larger, was ridiculed as a poor man's car. The Met's price was almost $300 less than the Willys Aero Lark, which, although a much larger automobile, was still viewed as a competitor in the small car field. Unlike either of those cars, the Metropolitan wore the badge, and halo, of Nash-Kelvinator, a long standing automobile company with a solid reputation.

Nash, of course, issued a press release announcing the car. The release, dated March 18th, began: "Nash Motors today unveiled its Metropolitan, completing 11 years of research and planning unparalleled in American automotive history." In the release, Sales Vice-President Henry Doss, stretching perhaps to properly express the unique character of the Met, stated: " ...the Metropolitan was developed in contradiction to the custom traditions and methods prevailing in the automobile industry. No small car of this type has ever been built before in this country or abroad. It is the first time that the most economical form of auto transportation has been built up to the standards required by the American auto owner in the matter of quality, performance, economy, comfort, and appearance.... It is the first time a completely new car was designed with the public as a partner."

Meade Moore, now vice-president in charge of Nash Research & Engineering, was quoted as saying,

"the basic purpose behind the long and patient research was to establish the validity of Mr. Mason's belief that all previous attempts at small cars in this country were failures because of the effort to 'squeeze down' a normal size car to small car proportions. He believed that the opposite approach might be successful. So Nash engineers began with the simplest and most efficient basic transportation and developed it up to the standards of beauty and performance that Americans have always demanded."

Doss, attempting to be sensitive to womens' needs (at least in the context of that era) comes off sounding slightly sexist today when he said the Met "provides a discriminating answer for the suburban housewife whose obligations now include being chauffeur and purchasing agent."

One rather interesting idea was to have the Metropolitan displayed in department stores since, as one executive noted "...remember—the Metropolitan

Popular Mechanics' Arthur Railton wrote: "There's a new Baby on Automobile Row" in April 1954.

California Met owner took this photo in Oahu, Hawaii, just after reluctantly selling his car. He wrote to Jim Watson: "Note The Crying Towel!"

makes downtown shopping practical because of its maneuverability." Zone managers were provided with a list, drawn up by Kelvinator, of department stores that would be good prospects for in-store displays.

It all worked to the good. All the elements of the Met design program merged together to form an automotive package the public could accept, and initial sales results were surprisingly good. The Nash marketing men had predicted well: a good number of people just wanted something different and many of them wanted to be the first in their neighborhoods with a Met. Even better news (for the retailers, at least): Nash dealers could earn a fairly good profit at the Met's suggested retail price, an amount just shy of $300 per car. And even higher profits were available by selling optional equipment, which included antifreeze for $1.25 extra (!), the Weather Eye heater for $64.15, AM radio for $55.80 and whitewall tires for $16.70 per set.

In that car-crazy decade any all-new car was bound to attract a great amount of attention from the press and the Met was no exception. The Metropolitan appeared on the cover of the April 1954 issue of *Popular Mechanics* (still, by the way, wearing an NKI badge!).

The Metropolitan was the choice of many women—it was economical yet fun to drive.

The Met was also featured on the cover of the April issue of *Popular Science*. *Mechanics Illustrated* published its own road test report that same month.

Road testers of the day fairly raved about the newest Nash. *Popular Mechanics'* Arthur Railton wrote, "There's a new baby on Automobile Row. It weighs about 1,800 pounds. The biggest thing about it is its name—the Metropolitan." Railton went on to explain that "In a two-car family, it is perfect as the second car," noting however, "But Nash (even after a careful survey) hesitates to define the market for its new baby. "They are," Nash says, just "feeling it out." Railton also admitted that the car was rather small. "It is tiny, all right, tiny but not ridiculous. In fact, the universal comment seems to be that "it's as cute as a bug." Cute as a bug? That wasn't exactly a great compliment in the Fifties but it was a fair one. Anyway, a Bug of a different nature was going to be its competition in the future, so it couldn't hurt to have a leg up on cuteness, could it? *Motor Trend* magazines' Don MacDonald hit the nail on the head when he wrote: " ...Nash has come up with a mighty mite good enough to seriously dent American prejudice against small utility cars." After explaining the Met was a British import, he noted, "The car is recognizable to both engineer and casual observer as a Wisconsin-born idea. After driving it around we find it a scaled-down version of everything good in a Nash, which is saying plenty." *Motor Life* may have given the Met its greatest compliment when it gushed, "We have never, at this writing, encountered a car which combined as many desirable features as does the Nash Metropolitan. We rate it good to superior in handling, roadability, economy, and traffic acceleration...the Nash Metropolitan is an excellent buy." In other words, they liked it.

Motorsport magazine headlined its July/August 1954 issue "Mighty Metropolitan—the new Nash small car packs a pleasant surprise in its handling-performance," and summed up a generally upbeat article by saying: "I'll guarantee you one thing. The new Metropolitan puts plenty of fun into driving and that in itself is worth the price of purchase!"

Twenty-four Hudson Metropolitans lined up for a dealer driveaway.

Here it is...
THE CAR THAT
Gives so much ... costs so litt

THE HUDSON METROPOLITA

American Styling . . . British Built . . . that's the Hudson Metropolitan— newest member of the famous Hudson family. Here is eager, alert styling that catches the eye immediately . . . styling that combines streamlined beauty with relax-as-you-ride comfort. Here is ruggedness that stems from its built-in-Britain origin plus real economy of operation.

The Hudson Metropolitan is a *quality* car from bumper to bumper. Powered by the famous Austin A-40 overhead valve engine, the Metropolitan responds swiftly to YOUR slightest wish. It's a "natural" for women drivers . . . so easy to handle, so easy to park.

Choose either the Hardtop or the Convertible in gleaming colours— then drive proudly, economically, distinctively in your Hudson Metropolitan.

So compact—so lovely—so packed with power . . . with styling women desire. The Hudson Metropolitan is des and built to go places smart economically. An ideal seco car for a busy family, too.

YOUR HUDSON DEALER WILL BE HAPPY TO ARRANGE A METROPOLITAN DEMONSTRATION ANYTIME AT YOUR CONVENIENCE

The Hudson Metropolitan's famous Austin A-4 overhead-valve engine easily whisks it along at top legal speeds . . . and it delivers up to 40 mi per gallon of gas. The Hudson Unitized Construction gives extra safety, extra strength, longer rattle-free life combined with clever Continental styling.

By mid-1954 Hudson dealers had the 1954 Hudson Metropolitan to sell. Note Hudson grille badge, "M" hub-caps and exaggerated "Metropolitan" name-plate on fender.

Women love this easy-to-handle Princess of the road. *Standard* equipment includes such *extra* luxuries as a radio, Weather-Eye Conditioned Air System, directional signals, continental rear tire mount, two inside sun visors, cigarette lighter, foam cushions and nylon-and-leather upholstery.

What a car! Here is the automobile that truly "Gives So Much— Costs So Little!" To see it is to want to drive it... to drive it is to want to own it.

Here's a car that really means business—you get more "go" with each gallon of gas ... cinch to park ... perfect for business use.

It's the right car for young couples on slim budgets—or for business women, nurses, and school teachers, or for anybody who wants a "classic" car that costs so little to run.

Mason and Romney were pleased. For an extremely small investment, they were able to offer an exciting new model, one that fit well in their small car lineup. The Rambler line of cars was beginning to slowly move up the ladder in size and market appeal that year with the addition of four-door sedan and station wagon models on a longer 108 inch wheelbase. Although the smaller 100 inch wheelbase Rambler two-door would continue for another year, the mainstay of the Rambler line was going to be the four-door station wagon with strong sales also expected from the four-door sedans. All of this meant there should be enough room at the bottom of the Nash product line for the low-priced Met.

AMC designer Bill Reddig bought one of the Engineering Department's Metropolitan test cars, a special one that had been equipped with overdrive. Reddig loved the car, which he bragged could "go all day on a cup full of gas." He sent the car over to one of AMC's engineering shops and had them install a handmade fiberglass trunk lid on the rear deck. Today, the whereabouts of Reddig's Met are unknown but it would be a real find for some lucky collector: it's one of perhaps only two Mets that AMC equipped with overdrive, and its fiberglass decklid is unique.

Nash General Sales Manager Jim Watson wasn't able to fully savor the Met's first year on the market. In May of 1954 he came down with an illness that was later diagnosed as a damaged optic nerve. He had no choice but to take a long term leave of absence at what turned out to be a critical time both for Nash-Kelvinator and for his own career.

This was also the year of perhaps the greatest changes to the ranks of the American independent automakers and among those affected most was Nash-Kelvinator. After many months of talks, it was announced that Nash-Kelvinator and the Hudson Motor Car Company would merge, effective May 1, 1954, into a new company to be called American Motors Corporation. In actuality, Nash was buying out the tattered remnants of the once mighty Hudson, in hopes it could consolidate Nash and Hudson automaking in its own Kenosha, Wisconsin, plant, meld the Hudson sales organization with the Nash organization and thus reap the cost savings and economies of scale of joint volume production. The Detroit-built Hudson line of cars was dropped at the end of the 1954 selling season, to be replaced by a line of Nash-based Hudsons introduced for 1955.

The Hudson dealer group, accustomed to selling (alongside its more modestly powered family cars) the high-powered Hudson Hornet (darling of the stock car racing crowd) suddenly found itself offering a line of Hudson Ramblers and, in the lowest price range, the new Hudson Metropolitan. Actually, the new Met jumped the gun on the rest of the revamped line of Hudsons, since it was first available at Hudson dealers as a 1954 model! The Hudson Metropolitan was identical to the Nash Metropolitan except that a Hudson badge in its grille replaced the Nash emblem. Reportedly, some were also fitted at zone offices with Hudson wheel covers, although by then the factory supposedly was fitting "M" badged hubcaps on all Mets. The Hudson Metropolitan catalog shows drawings of the new car with Metropolitan nameplate script that appears much larger than the Nash version. This apparently was merely artistic license since a different size nameplate doesn't show up in actual photographs.

So the little Met now had a second distribution outlet. This caused hard feelings among some Nash dealers who now had new competitors selling cars that were basically identical to what they sold. But the net affect might be positive; the merger should strengthen the company and, in the Met's case anyway, more dealers selling meant more sales overall. The Met would end its first model year in America in good shape.

The Metropolitan now had two sales vice-presidents, since Nash Metropolitan sales came under the direction of Nash Sales Vice-President Henry Doss, and the Hudson badged models came under the aegis of Hudson Sales Vice-President Norman VanDerzee.

In October of that same year, George Mason, chairman of American Motors Corporation, fell ill quite suddenly and checked into Detroit's Harper Hospital. His old friend and protege George Romney, now executive vice-president of AMC, went to the hospital for a bedside visit. There were several important issues pending that Romney would have to deal with while Mason was recuperating, so the talk turned to business. They had yet to resolve the problem of finding

Couple met when a used Metropolitan convertible brought them together.

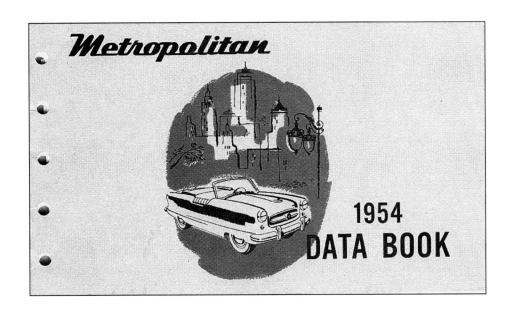

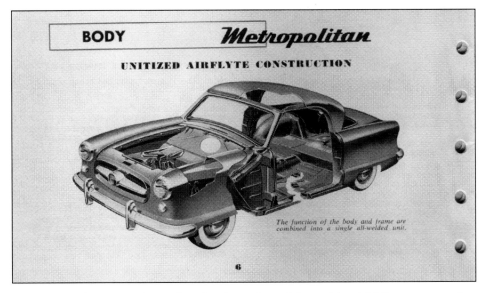

From the 1954 Metropolitan data book, a view of the unitized Airflyte construction.

someone to replace H.C.Doss as head of Nash sales. Although Jim Watson seemed promising, he had been out on sick leave five months already and it wasn't altogether certain that he would ever come back. They needed a new man at the head of Nash sales and he had to be brought on board soon. Mason knew of a sales executive in the Kaiser-Willys organization who sounded like the right person for the job. He and Romney discussed the man's qualifications, finally agreeing to offer him the job of Vice-President of Nash Sales. Romney said goodbye and left his boss. Mason seemed to be on the road to recovery. However, two days later his pancreas failed and he died. The Board of Directors elevated George Romney to Chairman of the Board, Chief Executive Officer and President of AMC the day after Mason's funeral.

Among the first of many details Romney attended to was to hire the sales executive that he and Mason had agreed on: the portly and gregarious Roy Abern-

ethy. He was known as a "dealer guy," one that dealers enjoyed working with and he seemed just the man AMC needed. Henry Doss soon retired. He and Vice-President Albert Wibel had been very much against Romney's and Mason's emphasis on small cars. After Mason died, Romney decided he wanted to keep only those executives who were willing to devote themselves to selling the company's full product line, small cars as well as large cars, and he had been unhappy with Doss' efforts. It's likely that Doss saw the handwriting on the wall and decided to leave while the choice was still his to make.

The year ended badly for AMC, with wholesale sales of Nash and Hudson cars down by over 100,000 units for the fiscal year, to just 135,794. Perhaps the only two bright spots were the new Metropolitan and the new longer wheelbase Ramblers.

The 1955 Metropolitan model year officially began on November 26, 1954. Any Metropolitans sold at re-

MERGER—Hudson President A. E. Barit, and Nash-Kelvinator Chairman George W. Mason, shake hands on merging Hudson and Nash. George Romney holds a plaque that shows the new corporate name, American Motors Corporation on May 1, 1954.

Popular Mechanics put the new Nash on its April 1954 cover. Note that this car still has the NKI Custom badges!

tail on or after that date were registered as 1955 models, regardless of when they had actually been built. This was easy enough for AMC to do since the Met was a low volume make and had virtually no appearance changes from its introductory year. In truth, it was a fairly common practice among some auto companies, especially in instances where the product's looks changed little year to year.

There was a new Metropolitan sales catalog for 1955 and its cover was a real beauty. A look inside, however, revealed that like the car itself, little was changed. The 1955 catalog was simply a reworked version of the '54. The name for the front suspension was now "Deep Coil Ride" rather than the prior year's "Airflex" name, while "Unitized Airflyte Construction" was now termed "Double Strength Single Unit Car Construction." Weights were listed about 50 pounds heavier, though why that was is unclear. The cooling system was now rated at eight quart capacity, up one-half quart from the prior year. The 1200cc engine was slightly modified and was now called the B series (the earlier version had been the A series). Of course, the company was now known as American Motors so some of the catalog wording was revised to reflect that. Probably more noteworthy was the cover photo. A beautiful picture in full color, it showcased the Met in a marketing niche AMC perceived it fitted well: as the second car in a two car family (the photo shows a big Nash in the garage), with a woman at the wheel.

The brochure was also updated to reflect the Met's first year sales success. The cover declared "40 Million Miles of Raves!," and was subtitled "The Amazing Success Story of America's Entirely New Kind of Car." Inside it trumpeted "The New Metropolitan Acclaimed by Thousands!."

Letters from satisfied Metropolitan owners were pouring into American Motors headquarters building on Plymouth Road in Detroit. AMC reprinted quips from a few of the letters in the catalog. A sampling: *"For years I have searched for a car that would give good mileage and economy, along with roadability, ease of handling and driver comfort. I have found it in the Metropolitan.... During May I drove 2,520 miles and averaged 38.2 mpg."* W.B.S. of New London, Connecticut, bragged: *"...I have enjoyed all sorts of fine, economical performance. Good riding - good steering - terrific mileage, both on a trip and around town."* T.C.D. of Pitman, New Jersey, reported: *"Since I have been driving the Metropolitan, I have been able to cut car op-*

erating costs in half." And A.S.S. (they should have watched those initials, shouldn't they?) of Richmond, Indiana, stated: *"I like my Metropolitan very much and—driving 60 and 65 miles an hour—I am getting 34 miles to the gallon of gas."*

Jim Watson finally returned to work on December 1, 1954, with the new title of Assistant Director of Dealer Development for the Nash Motors Division of AMC. It was unfortunate for him that his illness had lasted so long since it's likely he would have been a candidate to relieve Doss as head of Nash Sales. Roy Abernethy got the nod instead, so Watson was reassigned upon his return to AMC.

William Lee tested the 1955 Metropolitan for the April 1955 issue of *Car Life* magazine. Lee liked the Met, as most road testers invariably did, and wrote: *"Leg room is swell and the steering wheel and instrument panel just right."* To obtain the best acceleration figures, he advised drivers should *"Just pour it on gently but firmly and you'll have the youngster buzzing at 70 miles an hour long before many larger and more powerful cars reach 50."* Lee also loved the Met's parking ease, claiming he could *" ...slip this bit of machinery into any place big enough for a motorcycle-and-sidecar."*

Lee was thus merely agreeing with the vast majority of Met buyers. They sent AMC bags of letters praising the Met. For its part, American Motors was pleased it was enjoying such great critical success for such a small investment in product design and tooling. But realistically, this was the decade of the Fifties and AMC also realized the public expected to see new automobile features introduced nearly every year. The Met wasn't a mainstream competitor and couldn't hope to maintain its low price if it was re-tooled every two or three years such as the Big Three makes were. But a few improvements had already been investigated by Meade Moore and his engineering staff, and also by the people at Austin. There were some changes coming to improve the Met and they would be arriving in calendar year 1956. However, since this was a different sort of car, the model year changeover would be somewhat different from the norm.

The little Met would also accomplish something that many owners assumed was simply impossible; it would become a better and even more lovable car. For the Metropolitan, the best years were still to come.

Chapter Three

Improving The Breed (1956-1958)

Was there really any need to change the Metropolitan? That's a question that American Motors executives pondered in the mid-fifties and it's a question that automotive historians still ask. After all, the most successful imported car of the fifties and the sixties was the one that actually bragged about its lack of change—the Volkswagen Beetle. On the other hand, the Metropolitan was still just the number two selling import and perhaps with some alterations and improvements it might overtake the top car.

This was, of course, taking place during the first decade of Detroit's historic postwar horsepower race. Even traditionally conservative automobiles such as the Nash Ambassador were having their engines reworked to increase horsepower in an attempt to fulfill the seemingly insatiable desire of Americans for more power. Customers were clamoring for improved acceleration in virtually every automotive product but, in small cars at least, that same public also still expected excellent fuel economy.

There was a practical ceiling to all this, of course. AMC couldn't very well stuff a V-8 engine in the Met

(although at one point early in the concept stage Flajole did indeed suggest that route). To increase the engine size or power too much would simply ruin the fuel economy and/or the low price advantage of the Metropolitan. Besides, the little Met was never intended to be a hair shirt type of car; instead, it was supposed to be the automotive equivalent of bunny slippers; practical but also cute.

Although most of the magazine road testers had written approvingly in 1954 of the Met's power and performance, sales drooped somewhat in 1955. Austin earlier had approached the company with an idea of switching to a newer powerplant it had, one that offered improved performance. After the usual testing and negotiations (pricing had to be a big consideration, since a larger engine might require a larger transmission and rear axle, all of which might add too much cost to the product), a change was agreed on. Effective with early 1956 calendar year production, Metropolitans would be equipped with a new, larger engine.

Called the A-50, it was a good engine; it was a reliable cast iron four-cylinder with overhead valves and

Revised Metropolitan, dubbed the 1500 Series, debuted in 1956.

New Metropolitan 1500 Series featured new side moldings, two-tone paint even on convertible models.

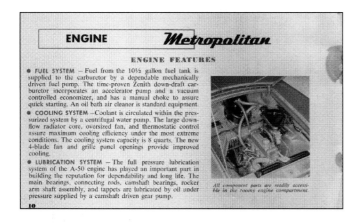

From the 1956 Metropolitan data book, a view of the engine and chassis features.

a displacement of 1500cc, up substantially from the earlier Met's 1200cc. Like the smaller engine, each of the new engines' pistons was fitted with four rings. The compression ratio, at 7.2:1, was the same as before. Also similar was the partial flow oil filter, available still as an extra cost option. The air filter again was a large oil-bath type and the choke mechanism was still manual. The new engine's rated horsepower was noticeably improved, as was its torque output. Torque was now 77 lb.-ft. @ 2500 rpm vs. the earlier engine's 62 lb.-ft. @ 2400 rpm. The new horsepower rating of 52 was only 10 more than the previous car

but when considered on a percentage basis, the improvement was 24 percent. Anything that's been improved by 24 percent is going to feel different, and the Metropolitan certainly did. In company tests, acceleration from 0-60 mph improved by a whopping four seconds, taking 22.2 seconds vs. the 1954 figure of 26.2 seconds. Top speed now was about 78 mph, up from 73. The overall roadability of the car, as several testers noted, was very much enhanced, peppier and more substantial. And oddly enough, the Met's fuel economy actually improved. American Motors tests revealed an increase of up to two miles per gallon of gas, the variance depending on the road speed it was measured at.

The clutch was new, a higher capacity eight-inch dry disc single plate type made by Borg and Beck, same supplier as before (previous clutches had been 7-1/4 inches). A running change on the earlier series of Mets had seen a switch to a hydraulically actuated clutch, and that feature was carried over onto the revised Met.

A new rear axle ratio was also introduced, 4.3:1, which permitted much quieter cruising than the earlier Met's 4.625:1 ratio. The new gear ratio also more than offset the fuel economy penalty usually expected from a larger engine, providing the improved mileage numbers noted.

Ride quality was improved by new shock absorbers. Tires, manufactured by Goodyear of England, remained the same size but now they were tubeless. As before, whitewalls were available at additional cost.

There were other changes as well. AMC decided to freshen the car's appearance with a bit of restyling. Not a whole lot could be changed. It was out of the question to alter the main body stampings since that would require expensive new tooling that would, in turn, drive up the cost and retail price of the Met. But a few minor updates were approved and they created quite a transformation in appearance. First was a new

1956 Nash Metropolitan hardtop, photo taken in Bridgeport, Connecticut.

Metropolitans, with more maneuverable size and excellent fuel economy, appealed to many women.

grille. The previous open grille (which featured an in-set floating bar, like the earlier Rambler) was replaced by a new style employing an oval-shaped opening framed in chrome, with a mesh grille insert. On the hood, the non-functional air scoop was deleted. Both of these alterations cleaned up the frontal appearance quite a bit more than the simplicity of the changes would suggest.

The biggest appearance change, however, was the switch in two-tone paint treatments. A new style was introduced that will probably remain in the public's mind forever as the definitive Met look. Someone in AMC Styling, it's not certain who, came up with new side moldings in a zigzag shape that served as the dividing lines for the revised two-tone paint. A design sketch, dated 1950 and drawn by Bill Flajole, clearly shows the same idea. However, a few persons are of the opinion that the design of the zigzag moldings was inspired by the 1955 Willys Aero. That's a point that's difficult to argue against since the similarity is obvious. The ex-chief of Willys sales, Roy Abernethy, was now a sales executive with American Motors. But nothing that definitely links the two molding treat-

ments has been found as of yet, so we'll only comment on how fortunate Met owners were to have such neat new styling.

Colors were revised as well. At introduction, there were just three color schemes available. The primary colors were now: P905 Caribbean Green, P910 Sunburst Yellow and P911 Coral Red, all of which were teamed with P909 Snowberry White on the lower body and for the hardtop roof. With the new moldings, even convertibles now were two-toned, unlike the first two model years. Convertibles came only with a black soft top, since tan was no longer offered. The mechanism for the soft top was revised to make raising and lowering it much easier. A new black vinyl cover was provided to enclose the top when it was in the lowered position.

Interiors also came in for some changes. Most noticeable was the seat upholstery; it was now a gray-black cloth (leather was no longer available) that featured a square pattern. This new material was similar to that used on some Nash Ambassador and Statesman models. The instrument panel, which in prior models was always painted the body color, was now

New gray and black upholstery with off-white vinyl trim was used in the interior of the new Metropolitan 1500.

painted black regardless of the exterior color. The Airflyte chrome script that adorned the ashtrays on earlier models was deleted. All in all, the interior might have seemed just a bit less deluxe than before, but it was still the classiest within its market segment.

New Metropolitan 1500 featured swanky looks, improved power.

The option list was expanded and now included a rather fancy hood ornament (probably designed by independent stylist George Petty), windshield washers, fuel filter, back-up lights, trunk light, curb feelers, visor vanity mirror, and outside rear view mirror, as well as the aforementioned partial flow oil filter. Naturally, the AM radio and Weather Eye heater were both still popular options, too.

The timetable for introducing the new car illustrates once again AMC's unconventional model change policy for the Metropolitan. The revised Mets wouldn't be put into production until January of 1956, thus couldn't be introduced until spring. But any unsold prior year models—that is to say leftover 1955s—would, because of company policy, be titled as 1956s beginning December 15, 1955. Thus, there would be two series of 1956 Metropolitans offered, leftovers equipped with the 1200cc engine and the revised series equipped with the 1500cc engine. There would also be, of course, the noticeable styling differences between the two models. It must have been confusing for any buyer who walked into a Nash or Hudson dealership that had both series in stock.

Two photos, sent in to AMC by an enthusiastic Met owner, show a puzzler—the car is a 1954-55 or early 1956 style 1200 but has the zigzag moldings from a later 1500 Series car.

The American Motors Product Planning and Information Department came up with a way to help avoid any confusion between the new 1500cc series and the older models. In the 1956 Metropolitan Model Information File they suggested denoting the new car by its engine size. They stated: "The designation, '1500' appears to be the most appropriate since the numerical reference immediately provides an identification for the new Metropolitan, and clearly separates it from the previous 1200cc models. This type of secondary identification has been used successfully in designating models of various firms. Examples as follows: MG-1500, Mercedes-Benz 300-SL, and the JaguarXK-140. The use of the term 1500 is opinioned to be especially necessary since the 1955 Metropolitans with the 1200cc powerplants have been licensed as 1956 models, on or after December 15, 1955."

Metropolitan 1500 it was, therefore, and just as before there would be only two models. The model designation numbers were also changed: the convertible was now the Model 561 and the hardtop was Model 562. The greatly improved Mets went into production during January of 1956.

The distribution pipeline was soon filled and dealers had a good inventory on hand for the public announcement of the Metropolitan 1500 series on April 9, 1956. A fairly substantial press kit was issued, necessary to adequately explain the numerous revisions to the car. The press kit included a comprehensive text that detailed the changes as well as the many other fine features of the car. On the inside cover of the press kit is an historically interesting "NOTE TO THE EDITOR." The note reads: "We'll appreciate it if you will avoid reference to the Metropolitan as the Nash Metropolitan or Hudson Metropolitan. Please use just Metropolitan or American Motors Metropolitan, Sold by Nash and Hudson dealers." The note is significant because it foreshadowed the coming changes to the AMC nameplates. Although in 1956 the Met was still badged as either a Nash or Hudson product, it was destined one day to become a brand in its own right and this minor note was the first indication of what was coming. At any rate, it was easy enough to avoid the marque names, since the press kit photos were shot at an angle that made reading the grille badge somewhat difficult anyway.

There was another change in the Met: the pricing. The suggested price was now $1,527 for the hardtop and $1,551 for the convertible, both up a bit from the 1954 introductory pricing, but not by much. At any

Mrs. Stanley Clark of Connecticut traded in a Packard hardtop when she purchased her Metropolitan.

Harold Hodges of Santa Ana, California, loaded up his Met for a trip to Niagara Falls that lasted seven weeks, during which he traveled over 7,000 miles and visited 16 states! Hodges wrote to AMC "the performance of this little car was terrific!"

America and added: "its greatest popularity is in suburban areas where its economical operation and ease of handling are big factors for those who must drive to the city and then park in congested areas. It also has reached great favor as a second car since it is ideal for driving children to school and making trips to the shopping centers. Another factor in its popularity is that it has a distinctive sports car appearance."

For all of the big guy's kind words, the market itself was tough for the independent makes that year and American Motors was locked in a struggle for its very existence. George Romney had launched a crash program to introduce a new Rambler for 1956 and that car was experiencing some teething problems. Money was getting scarce and the banks were tightening AMC's credit lines; in view of those problems, it's a wonder a new Met came out at all. But it did, and the press welcomed it with open arms and lavish praise.

Car Life magazine loved the larger engine, saying: "The extra performance resulting from this power increase makes the Metropolitan a very lively car that can easily keep up with the traffic flow on U.S. streets or superhighways." On *Car Life's* check rating scale, where five checkmarks is the highest score possible, the Met was rated five checks for economy and a respectable four checks for overall value for the dollar.

Motor Trend magazine was also complimentary, noting "American Motors' famous and ultra safe unit construction is used throughout." It noted that "two neat versions of this little car are available at an almost identical price … and incidentally, Metropolitan outsells all imports but Volkswagen." *Motor Trend* applauded the new engine, saying: "The Metro's powerplant may sound overworked at times, but it does an excellent job of pushing the 1,800 pound car (lighter than any other U.S. car) through traffic. Service is readily available from any Hudson or Nash dealer, at American prices." They summed up, under the rhetorical question "Why buy?" by calling the Met a "Best buy for low cost, second car operation … Good service more readily available than any other import…. Fine maneuverability, peppy performance." *Sports Car Illustrated*, perhaps not surprisingly, was much stingier in its praise, sniffing merely that "The current Metropolitan has few defects in the light car frame of reference." The few defects that it mentioned included seating capacity, wide turning radius and inaccessible luggage space, which were, in fact, shortcomings that were being mentioned more and more frequently by owners and road testers alike. The small car market was still in its infancy in America and the other imports suffered from much greater flaws than the Met's, so it was not a critical issue. Not yet.

AMC engineer Carl Chakmakian, the man who had wrung out some of the first Mets on a racetrack back in late 1953, also road tested the new Metropolitan and recalls, "I did a lot of running around with that one. [The revised Met] was … a real nice package, much better."

rate, it must be remembered that the standard equipment now included those new side moldings and fancy two-tone paint, as well as the bigger engine and various other improvements. And it was still a terrific price.

Big Roy Abernethy, now vice-president of automotive distribution and marketing, rattled off a few obligatory statements for the press. He noted the Met's position as the second best selling import in

Metropolitan Sales Manager, Jim Watson, called this "further proof of the ruggedness of the Metropolitan." The little Met suffered front end damage during a collision with what appears to be a 1956 Ford pickup. The Ford got the worst of it as it was knocked upside down!

Cover of Nash News announcing the 1500 series.

The Nash Motor Division of American Motors showed off the new Met on the front cover of its dealer newspaper, the *Nash News*. "Agile as a jackrabbit, easy to handle in traffic or on the highway, the smart newly-styled METROPOLITAN 1500 is a natural for cutting deep into foreign-car sales in America," it bragged. The new sales catalog for 1956 was headlined "Announcing the Amazing New, Blazing New Metropolitan 1500, with sparkling new power ... spirited new performance ... crisp new styling!" That same catalog introduced a new Met slogan that would become the one most recognized and utilized. It called the Met the "WORLD'S SMARTEST SMALLER CAR."

Well, it was smart, as in "smartly stylish." While most of its competitors were bland econo-boxes, the Met was stylish and light-hearted and fun. It was also, as the brochure said "Excitingly New and Different." The product team at American Motors had somehow come up with a product that seemed fresh, exciting and new, even though the sum of the overall changes was small.

NASH SALESMEN
MAY WIN COMPLETE WARDROBE

Many Nash dealers are assuring themselves of maximum sales volume by participating in the "Step-Up-Your-Sales—Step-Out-In-Style" salesmen's campaign. Every dealership salesman can win valuable clothing awards for each new car sale during "On Target"—Interwoven hose, Arrow shirts, silk neckties, Stetson hat, Johnson-Murphy shoes— even custom-tailored suits.

Salesmen! To get a complete wardrobe "on the house"—shoot the works now on demonstrations and appraisals. Make five personal contacts daily, at least 10 telephone contacts, send out 25 direct mail pieces every day during June.

STEP UP YOUR SALES
STEP OUT IN STYLE!

Sales promotion aimed at dressing up Nash salesmen.

METROPOLITAN IS THE SECOND LARGEST-SELLING IMPORTED CAR IN THE NATION

The foreign-built Metropolitan, comparatively a newcomer in the small-car field, already is giving "foreign-built" cars a real sales battle. In the past two years nearly 20,000 Metropolitans have been sold and today the sturdy little car is the second largest-selling imported car in the United States.

To strengthen its bid for a larger share of the market, the new "1500" boasts a brand new engine and broad styling changes. Nash dealers and salesmen have a unique product and an almost unlimited small-car market to shoot at for sales and profit.

NEW CAR REGISTRATIONS—FOREIGN CARS

	12 MONTHS 1955	PER CENT TOTAL
1. Volkswagon	28,907	49.14
2. METROPOLITAN	6,808	11.57
3. Jaguar	3,573	6.07
4. M. G.	3,001	5.10
5. Hillman	2,778	4.72
6. Ford	2,189	3.72
7. Austin-Healey	2,172	3.69
8. Austin	1,596	2.71
9. Porsche	1,450	2.46
10. Mercedes-Benz	1,364	2.32

Sales were good for the Metropolitan, but the rest of American Motors was in a state of extreme turmoil. Sales of the big Hudson and Nash models weren't good, and even the Rambler, the mainstay of the line, was experiencing an off year. The fiscal year ended with a loss for the company. But the Metropolitan program did receive some good news. James Watson, who had helped launch the original Met just before falling ill and taking an extended leave, was given a new position in the company. He had bounced around in various sales positions since his return to work in December of 1954, but in September of 1956, he was given a new title, one he would keep for as

Qualify Your Prospects!

Car Life magazine says using a 200-horsepower sedan weighing 4,000 pounds to carry a 125-pound mother and a 50-pound child two miles to school makes about as much sense as dusting crops with an intercontinental jet bomber.

There's a lot of "sales" truth and ammunition in that statement!

Qualify the people in your community—your neighbors, friends, business men, housewives, youngsters going to college, salesmen—there are scores of prospects right around you for the METROPOLITAN—as a first or second car.

The "Met" will pay for itself over and over in savings on gas, oil, tires and repairs.

Be sure to have a new "Met" on your showroom floor. Use your sales promotion material—window trim and posters, mat service ads, postcards, and line folders. Remember, you can't sell from an empty wagon. Make your dealership Nash headquarters in your town or city for the "Met"—distinctively different from all the rest.

PAGE 2

Nash News gave sales tips.

The "Amazing New, Blazing New Metropolitan 1500"—from the sales brochure.

long as there was a Metropolitan to be sold. Watson was now "Sales Manager-Metropolitans" for American Motors and he would become the Met's biggest promoter and its biggest fan.

Speaking of fans, letters were still pouring in to AMC from satisfied Met owners. Mr. J. H. Winters of California wrote: "After driving my Met for three months and 5,000 miles, I find more than 'looks' have been built into it. I get 38 to 40 miles a gallon. Now, it's no longer who gets to take the big car when my wife and I start to work—it's WHO HAS TO TAKE THE BIG CAR!" Hazel Baird of Vermont wrote: "In a trip to Albany, Georgia, we drove nearly 3,000 miles … and we averaged 40 miles a gallon!"

In April of 1956, Walker Bros., a big Nash dealer in Los Angeles, approached AMC with a plan to distribute the dealership's line of special Met accessories. These included a glovebox door, wind wings (side window air deflectors), steel spare tire cover, and rear fender skirts. Walker Bros. had been selling the items rather successfully themselves and was already wholesaling them to other Nash dealers.

Other news came about later in the year, with the availability of two new colors for the Met, Mardi Gras

Red, and Berkshire Green, both, of course, two-toned with white as the contrasting color.

Jim Watson kept pumping up the sales force. He had a small pamphlet distributed to salesmen that admonished them to "Get familiar with this Metropolitan Selling Slogan: THE WORLD'S SMARTEST SMALLER CAR! Tell it and You'll Sell." The booklet also suggested Met salesmen memorize a few "Key Metropolitan Selling Sentences." These sentences highlighted Met features in a general way, such as "Top Quality, Big-Car Safety, New Zip and Power."

The 1956 model year officially closed on October 24, 1956, its earliest finish yet. Any Metropolitans sold on and after October 25th were registered and titled as 1957s, regardless of when they were built. Of course, after such a thorough freshening for 1956, it wasn't expected that the Met would show much new for 1957, and it didn't. But there was a mighty big change that affected both the Metropolitan and its larger American cousin, the Rambler.

What the change entailed was dropping the Hudson and Nash brand names from both the Rambler and Met, allowing the two small cars to become individual makes on their own. Only the largest AMC cars would still be marketed under the Nash and Hudson brands, although the only Nash model now offered was the Ambassador and the sole Hudson was the Hornet. American Motors' volume brand name would be the one that George Romney termed "the car of the future"—the Rambler. Supplementing the Rambler would be the Metropolitan brand. Well, all of this had all been hinted at in the 1956 Metropolitan press kit, so it shouldn't have surprised anybody. For this one model year, though, AMC had four brands: Hudson, Nash, Metropolitan and Rambler.

The 1957 Metropolitan catalog was merely an updated version of the 1956 catalog, and it's difficult to tell them apart.

In January of 1957 the Fleet Sales Division of American Motors was pleased to report, in a memo sent to George Romney, that the little Met appeared to be catching on with utility companies. Fourteen seemed to be a common fleet number. Western Electric had fourteen Metropolitans in service, so did New York Telephone; Cincinnati & Suburban Bell also had fourteen Mets, all hardtops. The memo also reported that American Optical Company had three Mets in service, which replaced the motorcycles and scooters they formerly used.

During the first quarter of 1957 American Motors announced new pricing for the Met. Effective March 25th the Met hardtop would be priced at $1,567, and the convertible would be $1,591, at East Coast Ports

James Watson, Metropolitan sales manager.

Walker Bros. Nash dealership offered several Met dress-up items.

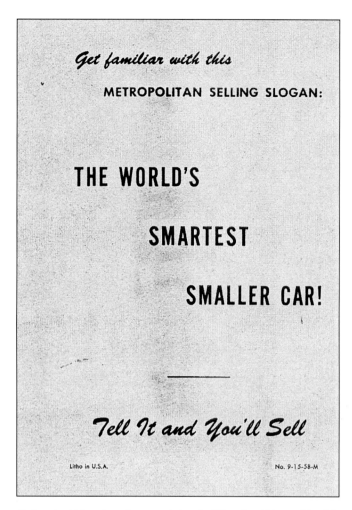

Get familiar with this

METROPOLITAN SELLING SLOGAN:

THE WORLD'S

SMARTEST

SMALLER CAR!

———

Tell It and You'll Sell

Litho in U.S.A.   No. 9-15-58-M

Sales training brochure advised, "Get familiar with this Metropolitan selling slogan."

Memorize

THESE METROPOLITAN SELLING SENTENCES

❶ **WORLD'S SMARTEST SMALLER CAR**—built in England, but designed for Americans. Serviced by over 2300 Nash and Hudson dealers everywhere.

❷ **TOP QUALITY** in a smaller package.

❸ **SMALLER CAR WITH BIG-CAR SAFETY.** All-welded single-unit construction makes it twice as strong, rattle-free, longer-lived, and far safer.

❹ **SMALLER CAR WITH BIG-CAR COMFORT,** results from its exclusive suspension. Rides smoothly over any kind of road.

❺ **EXCELLENT HANDLING AND MANEUVERABILITY.** It turns short, parks, and steers easily.

❻ **IMPORTED-CAR ECONOMY.** It delivers up to 40 miles to a gallon, on regular gas. Saves oil, too . . . and even the tires cost less.

❼ **NEW ZIP AND POWER,** with the new, stepped-up Austin A-50 engine. It takes off faster from stoplights. It has performance for turnpike speeds.

❽ **PLENTY OF ROOM FOR DAILY DRIVING,** with room for two adults and two youngsters and lots of space for groceries and other shopping items.

❾ **DRIVE TWO FOR THE PRICE OF ONE BIG CAR.** Actual figures show that you can buy and operate two Metropolitans for less than one high-priced big car.

What to say to sell a Met—advice from a salesman's guide.

For 1957, Metropolitan became a separate make. Note front marker plate displays model year.

This Met owner wrote to AMC that her car "costs me less than $1 a week to run it."

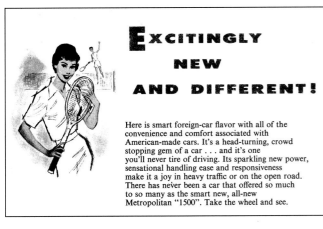

EXCITINGLY NEW AND DIFFERENT!

Here is smart foreign-car flavor with all of the convenience and comfort associated with American-made cars. It's a head-turning, crowd stopping gem of a car . . . and it's one you'll never tire of driving. Its sparkling new power, sensational handling ease and responsiveness make it a joy in heavy traffic or on the open road. There has never been a car that offered so much to so many as the smart new, all-new Metropolitan "1500". Take the wheel and see.

From the 1957 catalog: Met's appeal to women was understandable—low price, good handling and great fuel economy.

of Entry (POE). West Coast cars would be $42 higher, reflecting higher shipping costs.

Discussions were held to decide future product directions. One proposal was for a station wagon version of the Metropolitan. Another proposal, preferred by Romney, was to reintroduce the small Rambler two-door, which had been discontinued after 1955. It made a lot of sense to go with the latter, since most of the old tooling could be used, and of course that tooling was already bought and paid for. The resulting low amortization costs would allow a low price to be offered.

The 1957 Met saw few product changes of any real consequence. The contrasting white paint was changed part way through the model year to a new P914 Frost White, and reportedly the cigarette lighter was altered somewhat—and that was about it. But Jim Watson was the Met's sales manager and he was a capable fellow. Regardless of the lack of change in the product, Watson would create excitement.

1957 Metropolitan convertible.

Metropolitan Sales Manager Jim Watson sings Met praises to a prospect at an auto show.

One of Watson's best efforts to build excitement for his little car was the creation of a club for Met owners. Realizing, perhaps, that his advertising budget was too small to make any sort of a big noise in the marketplace, Watson decided to try for the oldest (and some would still say the best) form of advertising: word of mouth. The best way to link up with Met customers and build on their enthusiasm and camaraderie, might be to form a club for Met owners. Under Watson's plan, every purchaser of a new Metropolitan was automatically eligible to become a member of the Metropolitan Owners Club. Simply by filling out a form and mailing it to AMC headquarters, a Met owner would receive a membership card, a handsome grille medallion and a subscription to the Metropolitan Club bulletin, called *The Met Letter*. The Met magazine featured photos, letters and articles about Met owners and their cars. At the same time it encouraged a philosophy of thrift in all aspects of consumerism, including automobile ownership. The club's motto, *Motores Prudentiores*, (More Intelligent Motoring) summed it all up. Met owners who joined

A happy man, Jim Watson with Met convertible, circa 1957. Note Michigan license plate and Met Club emblem.

James Watson was the Met's greatest booster.

the club often found themselves becoming even more enthusiastic, tooting horns and flashing headlights in recognition whenever they saw fellow Met owners. The club bulletin carried letters from Met enthusiasts, recounting the adventures they had with their Mets, often including amateur photos of themselves and their cars. It was all great fun.

One rather interesting buyer who wrote to Watson was Mr. Charles Addison, a manufacturer of amusement park rides. Addison sent in his membership application along with a picture of a Metropolitan that his company had converted into a kiddy car fire truck! Mr. Addison bragged to Watson "the chassis is plenty strong enough to support the loads we haul and the motor has adequate reserve power to pull the trailer over all kinds of terrain." Evidently, Met fire trucks were sold to several amusement parks in New England and New York state at a delivered price of about $3,800 each.

For a promotion, this Metropolitan was man-handled into a Ventura County, California, bank lobby.

The Met fire truck in action!

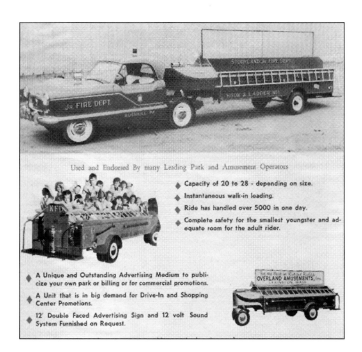

This owner hauled his boat with his trusty Met hardtop.

Advertisement for Metropolitan "tractor-trailer fire engine" amusement ride.

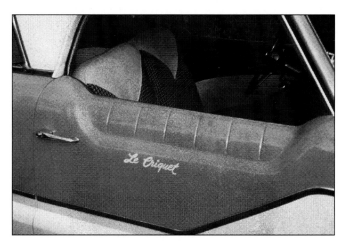

A Chicago-area Met owner dubbed his car "Le Criquet."

Miss Minamarie Goodwin of Arkansas drove herself and four friends to and from college in her Met hardtop, circa 1958.

Met owner Phillip Beatty designed a special trunk rack for his car.

Overall, the Metropolitan was having a good year. In a letter dated May 1, 1957, Watson wrote to a potential customer: "As you may have surmised we have been in very short supply of Metropolitans across the country since late last fall as a result of a substantial increase in the demand for this type of vehicle. Despite our doubling the production rate since last fall we still—in most areas—have not been able to provide much more than half the number of cars

cars was growing rapidly and that was proving a godsend for American Motors and the Met. Smaller cars were still a relatively new item to most Americans, and for a great many prospects the local AMC dealer probably seemed like the smartest place to shop. In addition, the public's response to the Met 1500 series was very favorable, and demand was growing.

The press was still in love with the Met, too, and that was spurring sales. The automotive editor for

George Romney and George Bush's Dad

American Motors Chairman George Romney was never a shy man when it came to sales. When Senator Prescott Bush of Connecticut, the father of future U.S. President George Bush, mentioned in a speech the need for smaller and more economical cars, Romney fired off a letter to him in Washington, D.C. To quote selectively from Romney's letter, dated April 22, 1957:

American Motors has been the leading exponent in this country of small and compact economy cars.... Early in 1954 we publicly introduced the 85 inch wheelbase Metropolitan, a four-cylinder car manufactured in England to our designs and specifications. This vehicle will yield up to 40 miles per gallon under ideal driving conditions. Because of your interest in gasoline economy, I have asked Mr. Harlan Walters of our Washington office to contact you and to provide you with additional facts about our economy cars that might be of interest. We are also asking Mr. Walters to arrange for you to take a demonstration ride in either a Rambler or Metropolitan at your convenience.

Sincerely,

George Romney.

It's recorded that Mr. Walters, AMC's Washington lobbyist, met with Senator Bush and even gave him a copy of a Met booklet titled *Are You Burning Your Money?* An offer was made for the honorable Mr. Bush to test-drive whichever AMC products he wished. Whether Mr. Walters' efforts resulted in a sale or not is unknown at this writing.

Booklet asked prospects "Are you burning your money?"

requested by our various zones."

Part of the problem of low inventories was that American Motors itself was seeing a large increase in sales of the Rambler and as the public's interest in the Rambler increased, it was driving up demand for the Met as well. Probably many of the new prospects showing up at dealerships hadn't intended on shopping there until the overall excitement with the Ramblers had drawn their attention. The market for smaller

the *Cleveland Plain Dealer*, Harry Linge, wrote: "A couple hours spent in driving American Motors' imported Metropolitan 1500 reveals why this sprightly little automobile gains new heights of popularity month after month. The Met is handsome, comfortable, peppy, and economical." *Sports Car Illustrated* proved it had warmed up considerably to the Met when, in a May 1957 article, it said: "Its behavior in the crowded city is nothing short of phenomenal

Metropolitan convertible in a lovely setting.

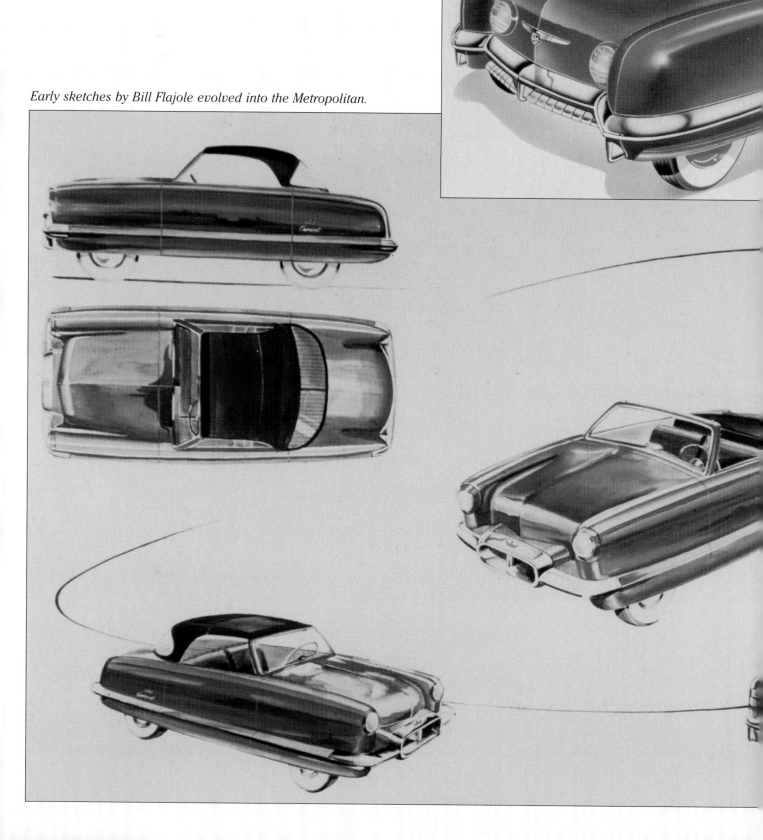

Early sketch by Bill Flajole bears Fiat nameplate and script lettering that appears to spell 'Esquire'.

Early sketches by Bill Flajole evolved into the Metropolitan.

Early sketch by Bill Flajole bears "1951" license plate, and was probably drawn in 1948 or 1949. Chrome letters on side appear to spell 'CROWN'. Note interesting rear window treatment and rear bumper.

Scale model of original NXI that evolved into Metropolitan.

Metropolitan convertible was a spunky car for moms.

Handsome designer Bill Flajole at the wheel of an NXI prototype.

Metropolitan hardtop was sensible, economical transportation for any businessman.

Beautiful 1956 Hudson Metropolitan.

The owner of this Met 'customized' it with tailfins.

This solid blue Met hardtop is a 'Jim Fisk Special'. Note non-original wheel covers.

Austin version of the Met 1500. Note right-hand steering.

Metropolitans appealed to both young and old!

Only color photo found thus far of rare maroon Royal Runabout show car.

Metropolitan made the front cover of Popular Science *April 1954 issue.*

Until recently it was believed that no color pictures of the Metropolitan Fifth Avenue survived. However, thanks to Guy Hadsall, we are able to display these beautiful pictures of a wonderful show car! Pictured are Jim Watson and an unidentified narrator.

Black Royal Runabout hardtop in its natural element — an auto show.

Black Royal Runabout hardtop show car, now in the Chrysler Historical Collection, had a fancy interior, single-tone paint.

The fabulous Met Westerner!

Met Westerner was a beautiful show car.

Look at those seats! Met Westerner had handsome, custom interior.

Side view of the Met Westerner shows script and cowgirl 'badge'.

Beautiful view of the yellow Metropolitan Royal Runabout show car.

Metropolitan once owned by Paul Newman and Joanne Woodward.

Met owners loved their cars!

Another bank promotion, this one in the Liberty Trust Bank in Cumberland, Maryland, in 1957. The Met was small enough to be used for such attention-getting promotions.

The Metropolitan Club Emblem!

The Metropolitan Club had it own "coat of arms": The Met Club Emblem. Many people have seen this medallion on Mets or pictured in magazines, and many have wondered at the significance of the symbols carried on it. Jim Watson explained it this way:

"If you will refer to your certificate of membership on which are listed the 'planks' in the official platform of the club you will note that the #1 plank is 'The conservation of vital natural resources, such as iron, oil and rubber.' The oil derrick on the emblem is symbolic of the conservation of the natural resource oil.

"The ore boat and the power shovel bucket are symbolic of the natural resource iron ore. The … rubber tree and the sap bucket … are symbolic of the conservation of the natural resource rubber.

The remaining symbol—the bank book—is symbolic of the #2 plank in the platform, 'The reduction of personal motoring costs—both capital and operating—thus making additional funds available to car owners to be used for whatever purpose they may desire … including savings. The bank book is directly symbolic of the monetary savings that the ownership and operation of the Metropolitan effect."

without engine falter or excessive second gear noise." *Sports Car Illustrated* went on to note: "Seats are high and firm and vision all around is excellent…. Interior appointments are nicely finished."

American Motors was finally on the move. Its volume car, the 108 inch wheelbase Rambler, was picking up steam in the marketplace. In Detroit, AMC's Kelvinator Division was displaying a radical product from its experimental labs. The device was an oven

This photo bears the inscription: "Two 'Met' Belles."

when compared with the lumbering hulks powered and geared for speed on the highway. It darts nimbly in and out of traffic with no strain or pain, and squeezes through the most unlikely openings while the giants sit immobilized by their own bulkiness. Gearbox and final drive are ideally suited to around town driving…. The latitude of second gear is nothing short of amazing. It can wind out to 57 mph and then some

This British market Austin Metropolitan appears to have single tone (monotone) paint despite having the zigzag moldings.

Harry Stanton, automobile editor for the Boston Globe with his own Metropolitan, at American Motors headquarters.

Stanton had a great affection for his Met, as evidenced here.

Harry Stanton, Boston Globe automotive editor, talks about his Met with Jim Watson. Stanton's Met reportedly was equipped with overdrive!

that, amazingly, cooked by microwaves! It was only a demonstration model, though. Some years would pass before it could be sold to the public. (Who would have guessed back then how ubiquitous the microwave oven would eventually become?) But AMC had something else it was working on and it was planned for a 1958 introduction. Because of the soaring demand for smaller cars, George Romney had decided to put the smaller 100-inch wheelbase Rambler two-door, last sold in the 1955 model year, back into

the reborn compact. Jim Watson had what he felt was an excellent idea. He suggested in a memo to Roy Abernethy "to consider calling this model the Metamerican—or Met-American." Watson explained, "Metamerican is made up of five syllables, the same as Metropolitan, and the two names would go together very well not only in pronunciation, but also in typographical setup." Watson then explained how the name would help identify the product as American made. But an addendum he added to the letter ends

Floyd Clymer Tests the Met!

Floyd Clymer, at that time the world's largest publisher of automotive books as well as being a longtime veteran of the auto industry, was intrigued by the Met. He decided, in 1957, to give the Metropolitan a road test. He arranged through Jim Watson to pick up a Met hardtop in Chicago for an extended test drive out West. Of course, high speed, long distance travel wasn't really what the Met was intended for, so such a test really wasn't a fair examination of the little commuter. It would be a strenuous workout. What's more, Clymer was planning to make the test even harder. He proposed running the little Met clear up Pike's Peak, that 14,100 foot high bump in the road of central Colorado. Clymer had already made the trip scores of times, in various makes of cars, and he knew how tough it was on machinery. He considered the test a sure-fire way to separate the cream from the commonplace.

Clymer was pleasantly surprised by the Met. "The 85 inch wheelbase is quite short and yet the ride is surprisingly good," he wrote. "Cornering is far beyond expectations and the suspension system is well designed.... Not only is the front vision good but side and rear vision is also good." He looked forward to the Met's big test. "Directly west of Colorado Springs is the famous Pikes Peak, one of the most colorful and

scenic highways in the world...," he wrote. Clymer headed up the mountain, soon dropping down to second gear, and sometimes first, as the steep climb and thin air slowed down the Met. "Soon," he wrote, "we were winding through colorful trees and shrubbery and now and then the grades ease off, but there is a constant climb.... By the time I reached the halfway stopping point, Glen Cove, many cars were steaming and many were standing with hoods raised and the drivers were replenishing the water supply." Clymer's Met, however, didn't need to take on additional water and seemed to be handling the mountain with comparative ease! Getting back into the Met, Clymer continued to the top of Pike's Peak. "Soon we were in snow, and we found the weather getting much colder. Here we also passed timberline, where vegetation ceases. No trees or shrubbery will grow at this high altitude." The Metropolitan handled the job with no problems. Clymer later went on to Gallup, New Mexico, as well as other stops, with the entire trip lasting some 2,912 miles. What did he write after that journey? "I can not praise the Metropolitan too highly. It is a fascinating little car to drive, its performance is far better than one would expect, and the ride is likewise more comfortable than expected."

production. It made a great deal of sense to bring back the small Rambler, since it was large enough to appeal to family car buyers, yet compact enough to appeal to economy minded shoppers. A big advantage of the little Rambler was that it could offer automatic transmission as an option, a feature that was becoming increasingly popular with buyers. But perhaps the biggest advantage the new Rambler had was that it could be profitably built in the company's Kenosha, Wisconsin, plant. AMC executives were asked to come up with suggestions of what to name

up being much more interesting than even the main points of that message. "P.S.," he wrote, "The Metamerican might also lessen the possible shock resulting from our not having a four-passenger Metropolitan ready this fall as many of our dealers have been led to believe we would."

Watson was probably referring to a pair of Metropolitan station wagon prototypes that had been designed by AM Styling in Detroit. One prototype was built by Pinin Farina of Italy, while the other was done in the AM shops. These handsome little wagons would

James Watson and Floyd Clymer.

Watson and Clymer with a sturdy Metropolitan hardtop.

METROPOLITAN "500"

At first glance this appears to be a stock right-hand drive Austin Metropolitan, but a closer look at this brochure cover reveals the "M" on the hubcaps and grille badge are backwards. This is a left-hand drive car that was photographed and "converted" to RHD by the simple expedient of flipping the negative!

Sgt. John McGowan of the 2nd Royal Tank Regiment wrote: "Enclosed is a photo of my two town and country vehicles." Sgt. McGowan's Met is a right-hand drive model.

indeed have held four passengers and they appeared to have good sales potential. But in the end they were not put into production because AMC chose to invest its development dollars on reintroducing the small Rambler two-door. Additional information about the Met wagons can be found in the chapter "Mets That Might Have Been." More important for us to consider here is Watson's reference to dissatisfaction, among dealers, with the Met's limited seating capacity.

Another development of importance occurred in 1957 when Austin began selling its own version of the Metropolitan in England and other Commonwealth markets (except Canada, where it was sold by AMC). The U.K. market Met was different from the U.S. version in several ways. First, it was marketed as an Austin and appeared in its own sales folder and also in the Austin full line catalog. And, of course, it was right-hand drive for England and other right-hand drive markets. Chassis numbers didn't follow the same series as North American bound Mets. This has caused automotive historians no end of trouble, since it seems impossible to determine the exact number of Austin Mets produced.

Early style Met convertible has "customized" side treatment created by its owner to match his 1957 Rambler wagon.

This factory publicity photo is marked "1957 Casablanca Fashion Show." Note the Nash emblem in grille.

A Met at the golf course.

Of course, right-hand drive Mets were primarily for the right-hand drive markets of the world but that didn't necessarily mean they could be sent only there and no where else. There was a market for right-hand drive in the United States if someone was willing to look for it.

Stories of Met owners taking amazing trips were legion. Consider the King family of Ohio, as reported by Al Rothenberg in the *Cleveland News* during May of 1957. Mr. King decided to take his young family to Florida for what his wife told the reporter was "our first major trip since we were married eight years ago." During the trip they encountered no mechanical troubles whatsoever with the King's sturdy Met hardtop. A new 1957 model, it ran like a champ, despite the unusually large load it carried. This included Mr. King, whom the newspaper account stated "weighs about 280 pounds," and of course there was also his wife Ruth. And one suitcase. And their four children. That's right, six people in a two-passenger car. The children ranged in age from 2 to 7. The trip ran all of 2,450 miles, and Mr. King reported that he averaged better than 33 miles per gallon. Mrs. King, by the way, sat in the front seat, wearing a maternity dress because she was expecting her fifth child within three months. The return trip was even more crowded for the Kings since they brought back souvenirs, grapefruit, tangerines and a baby alligator!

Metropolitan 1500 at the British Motor Show, London, October 1957.

This Kentucky owner wrote of his Met, "I have enjoyed it very much." Note addition of fog lights to front.

In 1958, AMC introduced a one-piece rear window for the Met.

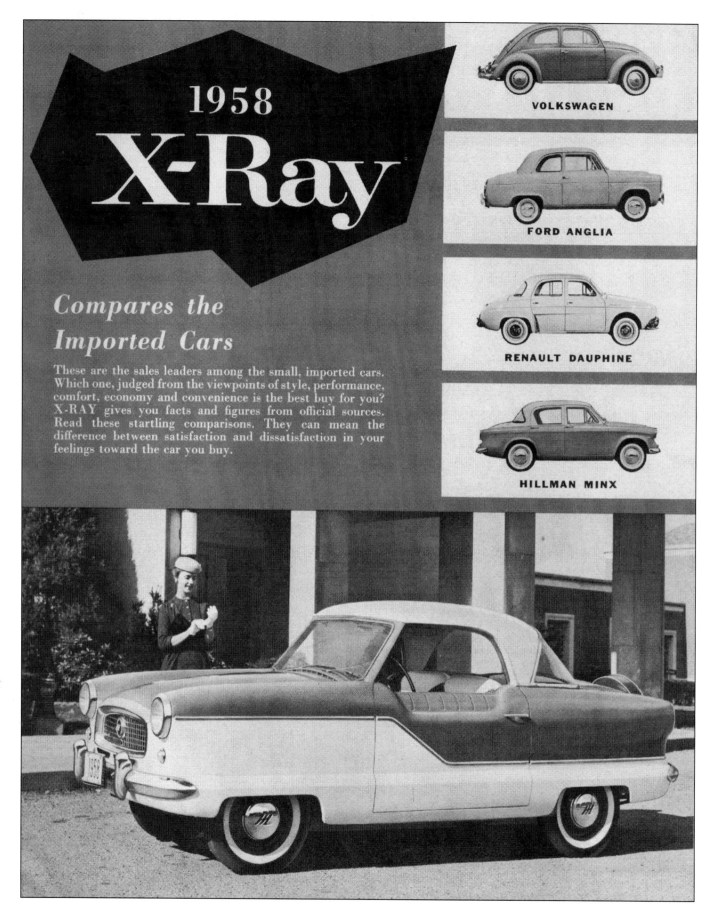

This 1958 X-Ray booklet compared Met with top European competition.

1958 Metropolitans stored deep in the hold of a transport ship.

This photo was sent to AMC with the following remarks: "I believe I have the nicest airplane and the nicest car on the market. Sincerely, Betty McNabb, the Flying Medical Record Librarian."

Towards the end of the year the Met's engine was revised a bit. Compression was raised to 8.3:1 and horsepower went up to 55. The main and connecting rod bearings were improved for longer service life. Also included now was a full flow oil filter as standard equipment. The changes were effective with serial number E-43116 and were announced in a bulletin to dealers on January 22, 1958. The revised engine was dubbed the A-55.

The Metropolitan's 1957 model year ended on October 21, 1957, so any new Mets sold on and after October 22nd were registered as 1958 models. There were some small improvements coming for the 1958 Met but they were so subtle that most folks wouldn't notice them easily.

The biggest change for 1958 came with January production. The three-piece rear window was replaced by a one-piece, curved glass window. This cleaned up the rear styling a bit while also providing improved visibility. A few mechanical changes, a revised door lock and new handbrake assembly, were introduced to production as running changes during the year, but nothing of great importance was differ-

ent. A welcome improvement was the addition of a glovebox door as standard equipment.

New colors were also introduced. The color choices now were P912 Berkshire Green, P915 Autumn Yellow, P913 Mardi Gras Red, and P908 Classic Black, coupled with P914 Frost White as the contrasting shade. The previous Met sales catalog was updated yet again and reissued.

American Motors printed one of its popular X-Ray booklets for the 1958 Met. The X-Ray booklets were an AMC specialty and were meant to be used by shoppers as an aid to comparing AMC products with the competition. In the booklets, AMC presented selected product specifications for its products as well as the competition's, making it easier for folks to decide which car offered the best value. In the Metropolitan X-Ray booklet, the Met was compared to its primary import competitors, the Volkswagen, the English Ford Anglia, the French-built Renault Dauphine and the British Hillman Minx.

In comparisons of front seat room, comfort and convenience, the Met generally scored well, with its small size offset by the better quality of its materials as well as its more comprehensive standard equipment. Controls and appointments were considered superior to the other imports because the Mets were more American in design and thus more familiar to drivers. Most of the competition used bucket style seats rather than the Met's more popular bench style seat, and most also had a floor mounted shift lever even though most Americans preferred the Met's column type shifter. In terms of exterior styling, the Met obviously had it all over the competition.

Pricing was close. The Met's sticker of $1,650.10 (equipped with options) compared well with the Hillman's $1,699 and the Dauphine's $1,645 price tags. The Ford Anglia, at $1,539 and VW at $1,545, both managed to undercut the Met's price, but they came with interiors that were starkly appointed.

When it came to performance—that's to say the real 0-60 mph acceleration with the pedal to the floor type of performance—the Met absolutely slaughtered the competition. To 60 mph from rest was 12.6 seconds faster than the VW! The Met beat the Ford by 10.6 seconds and the Renault by 11.6 seconds. Even the second fastest of the comparison cars, the odd duck Hillman Minx, was 5.6 seconds slower to 60 mph. The Met was clearly the hot rod of economy imports and yet, even with this sizzling performance (we mean by 1958 standards of course), the Met delivered better fuel economy than all but the hoary

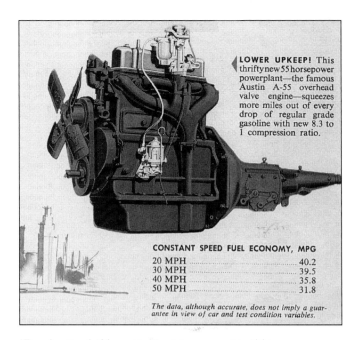

LOWER UPKEEP! This thrifty new 55 horsepower powerplant—the famous Austin A-55 overhead valve engine—squeezes more miles out of every drop of regular grade gasoline with new 8.3 to 1 compression ratio.

CONSTANT SPEED FUEL ECONOMY, MPG	
20 MPH	40.2
30 MPH	39.5
40 MPH	35.8
50 MPH	31.8

The data, although accurate, does not imply a guarantee in view of car and test condition variables.

The Austin A-55 engine had increased to 55 horsepower.

VW. And, as the X-Ray booklet warned: "the most serious drawback in buying some foreign cars is lack of adequate parts and service facilities. Most foreign car dealers are concentrated in relatively few states. That means that if you drive a foreign car in any of the

A California couple took this photo of their Met while traveling in Mexico during 1958.

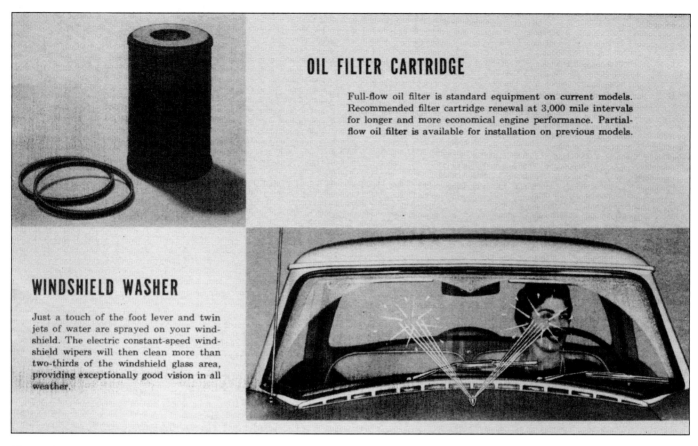

OIL FILTER CARTRIDGE

Full-flow oil filter is standard equipment on current models. Recommended filter cartridge renewal at 3,000 mile intervals for longer and more economical engine performance. Partial-flow oil filter is available for installation on previous models.

WINDSHIELD WASHER

Just a touch of the foot lever and twin jets of water are sprayed on your windshield. The electric constant-speed windshield wipers will then clean more than two-thirds of the windshield glass area, providing exceptionally good vision in all weather.

Views from the Met accessory catalog.

other states, you risk being stranded many miles from a dealer with parts and service for that car. Metropolitan service is available in all states."

The X-Ray booklet suggested "Before you buy any smaller imported car, by all means see and drive the Metropolitan. It offers luxury in miniature ... distinctive personal transportation for two people in either hardtop or convertible body styles. It is the World's Smartest Smaller Car."

The Louisville Pharmacy in Monroe, Louisiana, had this Met hardtop fitted with a large prescription bottle on the roof, and store name painted on body sides. The bottle lit up at night, creating an effect the owner termed "actually sensational."

Within that summary was the gist of what the Met's basic problem was: It could offer transportation for only two people. Certainly, many owners routinely traveled with three people squeezed onto the front seat and many others also regularly crowded children into the rear seat area, but neither of those practices was a use the Met was designed for. The Met was limited in the marketplace by its unique two-passenger design and that design would always restrict its sales potential.

But there were other potential uses! Radio station WPDM (1470 on the dial) of Potsdam, New York, had its station letters painted on the side of a Met convertible, thus making the car into a rolling (and highly visible) billboard advertisement. AMC began importing right-hand drive Mets into America and selling them to police departments for use in parking meter patrol. That usage was a bit out of character for the car but it was a nice bit of plus business for AMC. Potential Met buyers could reassure themselves that if the car was rugged enough for police use, it was rugged enough for the commute to work.

Meanwhile, AMC had introduced a new Rambler to its model range. This was the small 100 inch wheelbase car that Watson had suggested be named Met-American. In the end the company sensibly chose to capitalize on the name recognition and popularity of the Rambler brand. The new car was called the Rambler American to distinguish it from the regular 108-

Frederick Hartman, general manager of radio station WPDM, Potsdam, New York, had his station's call letters painted onto this Met.

inch wheelbase Rambler, which was AMC's "family" car. The Rambler American was nothing more than a face-lifted version of the earlier Nash and Hudson Rambler two-door, last sold in 1955 and discontinued at the end of that model year. Romney brought the small Rambler back to be able to offer a low priced family sedan at the bottom of his price range. The Metropolitan couldn't fill this spot and sell in sufficient volume because of two shortcomings: A) because it was a two seater, it was too small to appeal to a large section of the small car market and B) it didn't offer an automatic transmission, which was becoming increasingly popular with customers. The American had the advantage of being built with tooling that, for the most part, was bought and paid for long ago, fully amortized and thus saving much of the fixed cost of the car. AMC was able to price the revived Rambler at just $1,789 (for the Deluxe two-door sedan) and still make a decent profit. The American also had the advantage of being built in AMC's Kenosha, Wisconsin, factory. The much shorter pipeline of cars traveling from factory to market meant that the American could offer a broader range of options, including automatic transmission (which AMC called Flash-O-Matic), overdrive, reclining seats, and solex glass. The American could also be had in a fancier Super model.

As expected, the Hudson and Nash brand names were retired at the end of the 1957 model year. The two big AMC cars were replaced by the "Ambassador, by Rambler," which mounted the big Rambler's body on a longer 117 inch wheelbase. Discontinuation of the Hudson/Nash brands had been hinted at when the 1956 Mets were announced and by 1957, it surprised few. Notwithstanding, it was an extremely sad day for enthusiasts.

In January 1958, Watson received a photo of a Met hardtop operated by a baby sitting service. The company had its name and a cartoon picture of young

Met hardtop advertises Babysitting Service, circa 1958.

parents hand painted onto the Met's sides. The Met was being used as a rolling billboard more and more often and it was the perfect car for the job. Its cute style and economical manners were just what businesses needed.

Another market that held some potential was the "European Delivery Plan." This idea, which some other imports used, allowed a buyer to purchase a Metropolitan through his local dealer but take delivery of the car in Europe! The buyer could then tour Europe in his new car, saving himself the estimated $590 cost of renting a car while there. At the end of his European vacation, the buyer's new Met would be shipped to America, where he could then continue to enjoy the car for many years to come. This "Delivery Abroad" plan was espoused in a handsome brochure by a company called Continental Car Combine, situated then at 1741 Broadway, in New York City. Since the expense of renting or leasing a car in Europe was considerable, the unique purchase plan represented real savings. Admittedly, there was only a small number of potential buyers who could afford both a new Met and a European vacation at the same time, but the clever idea did manage to move a few extra cars.

In February of 1958, Jim Watson received a letter from a lady Met owner in Colorado. The woman was a nurse at a factory in Denver. She wrote: "My little

Colorado nurse loved her Met!

car's quite the talk out here at the plant. I get kidded about it, until I show the men its worth. Just today I brought in the pamphlet to give to a prospective buyer. They like my mileage. Those who live in my vicinity, a suburb of Denver, I bring them to work, rather, I let the guys drive it to work, and they are amazed. Then they understand why I am able to pass up the bigger cars. Every day I drive it I find another reason for liking it better."

The Whitefish Bay, Wisconsin, Police Department bought this Met to replace the motorcycle it formerly used for parking patrol, circa 1958.

"Hap" HOLIDAY saw all of Europe at substantial savings which paid his fare across, and is now the proud owner of

the Amazing New, Blazing New

METROPOLITAN "500"

SPECIAL DEAL FOR G.I. JOE

TO ALL EUROPE

MANUFACTURED BY B.M.C. (AUSTIN OF ENGLAND)
ON AMERICAN MOTORS CORP. SPECIFICATIONS (NASH-HUDSON)

THE C.C.C. "DELIVERY ABROAD" PLAN IS THE WISEST ONE! COMPARE THESE THREE PLANS . . . JUDGE FOR YOURSELF!

1) OVERSEAS PURCHASE FOR *UNLIMITED USE ABROAD, RETURN AND KEEP IN U.S.A.*

New Metropolitan Convertible with Radio and Heater, price at factory	$1450.00
(Hardtop $1375.00 only)	
Shipping charge to U.S.A.	110.00
Duty on C.C.C. Abroad Purchase (with $500 personal exemption, subject to customs regulations)	25.00
Your total investment	$1585.00
Competitor's charge for limited 3 months use of a less powerful convertible, under their "Purchase-Repurchase" Plan	$ 590.00*
You own a SMART METROPOLITAN back in U.S.A. for	$ 995.00
Present U.S. Delivery price (Coastal Price Lower)	$1850.00
Your total saving	$ 855.00

2) OVERSEAS PURCHASE FOR *UNLIMITED USE ABROAD & RESALE IN U.S.A.*

Actual investment of Metropolitan as above	$1585.00
Present U.S. Resale value approx.	$1550.00
Total cost of *unlimited* use of car abroad	$ 35.00
Saving over competitor's charge of $590.00	$ 555.00

3) OVERSEAS OUTRIGHT PURCHASE PRICE

Competitor's price at factory for less powerful convertible with heater and radio	$1790.00
Metropolitan price at factory with Weather Eye Heater and Radio	$1450.00
Saving in investment	$ 340.00

*Competitor's charge of $590 is based on their Repurchase at a depreciation of $450 plus cost of heater and radio, which are non-refundable.

PRICES SUBJECT TO CHANGE WITHOUT NOTICE

ADVANTAGES OF A CAR IN EUROPE

- See Old World's Obscure, Historic and *Romantic* places!
- Four can travel *for the price of one.*
- Hotels, meals, shopping are *less expensive away from tourist centers.*
- You go where, when, how you like *without delay for buses, trains or lost baggage.*
- You'll *see much more in comfort—spend far less in dollars.*

ADVANTAGES OF RESERVING A CAR HERE AND NOW

- Top *priority in model, color and time of delivery.*
- *Eliminate costly delays, disruption of your travel plans.*
- *Guaranteed on time delivery at place and date desired.*

ADVANTAGES OF THE BRITISH-BUILT METROPOLITAN

- *Dashing sportive, convertible or hardtop including radio and heater.*
- *Forty miles per gallon economy—large car comfort at lower cost.*
- *World wide spare parts abroad through B.M.C. (Austin-Healy, MG) American Motors dealers.*
- *Service and parts at home through your friendly neighborhood American Motors (Nash-Hudson) dealer.*
- *Savings on rentals, repurchase and tips—Pays for your car.*

C.C.C. FREE SERVICES

- CCC schedules *delivery anywhere in Europe.*
- CCC secures all international *traveling documents.*
- CCC obtains international *driving permit and auto club membership.*
- CCC *eliminates* necessity for $2,000 cash bond.
- CCC *arranges registration, insurance, and all troublesome details for you.*
- CCC *experts will advise on any travel problems.*

FINANCE PLAN AVAILABLE, IF DESIRED.

All Checks payable to

CONTINENTAL CAR COMBINE A. G.

1741 BROADWAY · NEW YORK 19, N. Y. · PLAZA 7-7790

European delivery was offered for Metropolitan.

Contrast the little Met with that big Buick in the background!

In April of 1958 AMC released several Product Analysis Reports to dealers. The PARs were similar to the X-Ray reports but were meant for dealer information. The Volkswagen sedan was again the primary target, no doubt because of its position as the best selling import in America. The VW sedan had a real price advantage of over $100 (approximately 6.5 percent less) when compared to the Met hardtop (assuming both were comparably equipped with radio, heater and whitewalls). In a comparison of convertible models, the Met had it all over the VW. The Met ragtop listed at $1,798.60 equipped with radio, heater and whitewall tires, while the VW convertible equipped similarly was $2,161.50! As the admittedly biased report noted: "Stylewise, the Volkswagen is over 26 years old." AMC went out on a limb by also comparing the Met hardtop to the Karmann Ghia coupe, stating that Volkswagen was merely "emulating the advance styling concept of the Metropoli-

tan...." As AMC noted, the Karmann Ghia "is priced about $900 above their two-door sedan." Although the VW was considered a decent riding car, due to its unique torsion bar front suspension, AMC suggested: "Of course, the best answer to this is to ride in the Metropolitan. Deep Coil Front Suspension has established its reliability on American roads and under American driving conditions."

AMC went further out on a limb, nearly breaking it, by comparing the Met convertible with Austin's popular MG-A sports car. The Met, when fully equipped, came out $838 less than the MG-A. This wasn't really startling news since they were dissimilar cars. Surprisingly though, the fuel economy of the two cars was nearly identical! The Met had a minuscule 1.5 mpg advantage (39.5 vs. 38 mpg) at a steady 38 mph, but the MG was actually two-tenths better at a steady 50 mph. Of course, both cars carried what was basically the same Austin 1500cc en-

Product Analysis Report

'58 COMPARISON REPORT NO. 1M — **DETROIT, APRIL 1, 1958**

1958 METROPOLITAN vs VOLKSWAGEN
ON VALUE . . . STYLING . . . PERFORMANCE

METROPOLITAN "1500" HARDTOP

VOLKSWAGEN SEDAN

COMPARE PRICES

	METROPOLITAN		VOLKSWAGEN			
	Hardtop	Convertible	Two-Door Sedan	Sliding Sun Roof Sedan	Convertible	Coupé Ghia-Karmann
A.D.P.*	$1626.10	$1650.10	$1545.00	$1625.00	$2045.00	$2445.00
Heater	69.00	69.00	STD Manifold Type	STD	STD	STD
Foam Rubber Cushion	STD	STD	NA	NA	NA	NA
Cigarette Lighter	STD	STD	4.50	4.50	4.50	4.50
Sun Visors	TWO	TWO	ONE	ONE	ONE	TWO
Directional Signals	STD	STD	STD	STD	STD	STD
Two-Tone Paint	STD	STD	NA	NA	NA	NA
Interior-Light	MAP	MAP	DOME	DOME	DOME	DOME
Dual Electric W/S Wipers	STD	STD	STD	STD	STD	STD
Oil Bath Air Cleaner	STD	STD	STD	STD	STD	STD
Oil Filter	STD	STD	12.00**	12.00**	12.00**	12.00**
Continental Tire Carrier	STD	STD	NA	NA	NA	NA
Sealed Beam Headlights	STD	STD	STD	STD	STD	STD
Radio and Antenna	61.55	61.55	70.00	70.00	70.00	70.00
Whitewall Tires	17.95	17.95	30.00	30.00	30.00	STD
ADJUSTED TOTAL	$1774.60	$1798.60	$1661.50	$1741.50	$2161.50	$2531.50

** Approximate Dealer Installed

METROPOLITAN SCORES ON VALUE...If comparable equipment such as foam rubber cushions, two-tone paint and continental tire carrier were available on both cars and price adjusted accordingly, Volkswagen prices would be appreciably more. For example Volkswagen dealers in extreme climates would recommend an optional gas heater priced at approximately $125.00 more.

*Notes: Based on Factory Delivered Price F.O.B. Port of Entry (New York) as of date of publication includes Federal Excise Tax and Import Duty. Does not include transportation charges, state and local taxes or optional equipment. According to the information available to us, Volkswagen-base prices are set by certain Volkswagen distributors at prices much higher than those quoted above. At West Coast Port of Entry Volkswagen delivered prices are up approximately $100 while Metropolitan prices are up $52.65.

It was Met vs. Volkswagen Beetle in this Product Analysis Report.

Product Analysis Report

'58 COMPARISON REPORT NO. 2M   DETROIT, APRIL 1, 1958

METROPOLITAN MATCHES MG-A ON MANY COUNTS....BUT COSTS $838.40* LESS

METRO CONVERTIBLE

MG-A

CONFIDENTIAL

The Metropolitan obviously is built for those who want good, dependable, economical performance, combined with the easy handling and maneuverability of a good sports car like the MG-A.

> This report is not to be taken as an attempt to draw a comparison between the MG-A and the Metropolitan. The MG is purely a sports car, while the Met is built primarily for convenience, economy and utility. Nevertheless, Metropolitan buyers can take pride in the fact that their cars not only compare favorably with the higher-priced MG-A in many ways, but actually are better in a number of important details, despite the more than $838.40* in price.

THE FACTS ON PRICE

ITEM	METROPOLITAN CONVERTIBLE	MG-A ROADSTER (DISC WHEELS)
Car	$1650.10	$2462.00
Radio with Manual Antenna	61.55	65.00*
Heater	69.00	65.00*
WSW Tires	17.95	45.00*
	$1798.60	$2637.00

Metropolitan A.D.P. Advantage, including options - $838.40

All prices shown are East Coast Port of Entry Delivered Prices EXCEPT items marked with an asterisk which are West Coast Port of Entry Delivered Prices. It is assumed on the items marked with an asterisk that East and West Coast Port of Entry Prices are identical.

*Eastern Port of Entry Delivered Price.

Met vs. MGA! Product Analysis Report, April 1958.

Product Analysis Report

'58 COMPARISON REPORT NO. 4M | DETROIT, APRIL 15, 1958

COMPARING METROPOLITAN WITH GM'S OPEL METROPOLITAN—DISTINCTIVE PERSONAL TRANSPORTATION

METROPOLITAN '1500'

OPEL REKORD

CONFIDENTIAL

Opel, GM's entry into compact car market appears to be pint sized '57 Buick. Opel Rekord is family size while Metropolitan provides distinctive modern transportation for two people plus. Metropolitan priced $332 lower, packs more performance, more zip and go in a more compact, more maneuverable car.

1957 BUICK

MET LISTS FOR $332 LESS THAN OPEL

List Price Port of Entry	Metropolitan '1500' 2-door Hardtop	Opel Olympia Rekord 2-door Sedan
(East Coast)	$1626.00	$1958.00

Included in the $1626.00 POE price for the Metropolitan are directional signals, electric windshield wipers, dual sun visors, two-tone paint, foam rubber front seat cushion, cigarette lighter and oil bath air cleaner. Add $69.00 to Metropolitan price for heater which is included in Opel price.

Product Analysis Report, April 1958.

Four Milwaukee Journal dispatch service Metropolitans.

Overseas distributor converted a Met to "delivery wagon" pictured.

gine, so perhaps those results shouldn't surprise anyone. The MG's engine was equipped to put out more horsepower (72 vs. the Met's 55 horsepower) because its primary market was sports car enthusiasts, not commuters.

Another comparison looked even more comical: the Met vs. the Opel Rekord. The Opel, as the report noted, looked like a shrunken 1957 Buick. The Met, of course, looked like a shrunken Nash Ambassador, so the pictures of the two comparison cars has a slightly surreal look. No matter. The Met compared very well, being 5.7 seconds faster to 60 mph, slightly better in fuel economy and a whopping $332 less costly. Evidently, the Opel's performance wasn't meant to emulate the 1957 Buick, because the Met proved to be superior hands down. This is probably why one still sees so many Mets nowadays. But when was the last time you saw a 1958 Opel Rekord?

One long distance correspondent sent a letter and photo to AMC from Okinawa, Japan. The picture showed a Met hardtop used by the Keystone Photo Service. This Met was modified by the addition of a rear "station wagon" plastic shell that was attached onto the rear deck of the car and replaced the regular rear window. The local AMC distributor there, Island Enterprises, stated that it hoped to produce additional conversions.

Met sales in 1958 were adequate but Watson felt the potential existed for even greater sales. Several product improvements were pushed through to eliminate a few items that consumers had found fault with. These would be ready for the 1959 models, which it was hoped would sell better than ever before. American Motors was now experiencing continuous growth and the demand for its small cars was red hot. The Met wasn't a mainstream product such as the popular Rambler American, but it could grab

Small Met ad from 1958 was aimed at women. Note "sold and serviced by Rambler dealers." Such tag lines blurred the Met's brand name distinction.

onto that car's coattails and go along for the ride. It would prove to be an exciting journey.

Small car fever was now running rampant throughout the country. Toward the end of the year a group representing 400 parking garage owners in New York City announced they would soon begin charging higher rates to owners of large cars. The name of the organization, quite coincidentally, was the Metropolitan Garage Board of Trade.

Chapter Four

The Road to the Top (1959-1960)

As the 1959 model year opened, there was news, both good and bad, for the little Metropolitan. The good news was that several noteworthy improvements had been made to the automobile, all of which came in answer to customer concerns and the sum of which would greatly enhance the sales appeal of the

From the Saturday Evening Post, December 1958, American Motors Chairman, George W. Romney, with youngest son Mitt. Note family Metropolitan in background.

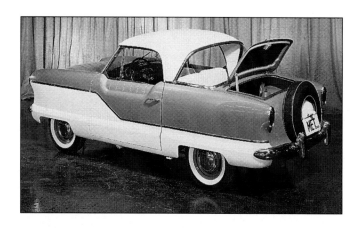

1959 Metropolitan hardtop offered smart styling, new outside opening trunk access.

lovable little machine. The bad news, not for AMC per se, but rather for the long-term viability of the Met, was first glimpsed when sales figures for the Rambler American were reported.

At the tail end of 1958 an interesting photo of George Romney and his young son Mitt, with Romney's Metropolitan parked in the background, appeared in a magazine article. Although he was by now one of the most famous businessmen in the world, Romney still chose to drive a variety of the company's automotive products, including the lowest priced ones, rather than limit himself to driving only the flagship Ambassador.

The Metropolitan's 1958 model year officially closed on October 7, 1958, so any new Mets sold on or after October 8th were titled as 1959 models. There was a change made in the steering system, introduced into production toward the end of the calendar year—hardly worth mentioning. A great deal more change was due to arrive shortly afterwards.

Luckily, historians today can track product changes to the Met simply by locating and reading the Metropolitan Model Information Files—short product reports that American Motors issued periodically. One such document, dated December 8, 1958, and written by that redoubtable AMC engineer Carl Chakmakian, detailed the upcoming revisions to the Met. To quote selectively from the file:

"Significant improvements will be made on the Metropolitan 1500, in accord with American Motors' design concept to improve the product without creating obsolescence due to non-functional changes. The improvements are considered as important sales features to attract consumers with a finer product more competitive with small foreign cars.

"The running changes are scheduled to be in production (in England) by mid-January 1959...."

The single most noticeable change, and the one that was most overdue, was the addition of an exterior trunk lid that served to greatly improve access to the rear storage area. In company discussions during the planning stage of this new feature, a suggestion was put forth that the fold down rear seat, which had formerly provided access to the trunk, be discontinued as a cost saving gesture. However, wiser heads prevailed and that useful feature was retained. It

For 1959, Met boasted an outside trunk lid.

Met convertible for 1959. Note vent windows.

For 1959, outside opening trunk was big news and American Motors showcased it in many press photos.

made perfect sense to include both accesses. A Met owner could use them to maximize trunk space by leaving the rear seat folded down to carry long items and using the trunk lid to ease sliding the items in. The rear seat key lock mechanism was replaced by a push-button key lock similar to the type used on the glovebox so that it wasn't necessary always to use a key to fold down the seat. The key would only be needed if the owner wished to lock the rear seat back. Chakmakian also noted that the "raised bead" that ran lengthwise down the center of the rear sheet metal, where the new lid was located, was eliminated to produce a neater appearance. The new deck lid took up most of the top of the rear area and featured two exterior chrome plated hinges, as well as a chrome plated turn handle, with a lock, for easy access.

Almost as noteworthy were the new side vent windows. A common complaint among Met owners was the less than ideal ventilation provisions of earlier production cars. On the earlier Mets, it seems that rolling the side windows part way down usually provided inadequate air circulation, while rolling them all the way down often gave too much! The big Nash dealer out in Los Angeles, Walker Bros., had offered a set of wind wings as a dealer installed option to help alleviate the problem, but AMC felt the devices just weren't enough and finally okayed the addition of vent windows as standard equipment. The new vents were of a simple push-pull design, much like the Rambler American's.

The Met also received larger tires as standard equipment, 5.60x13 replacing the former 5.20x13s. Chakmakian revealed his careful attention to detail when he informed the reader:

"Since the new 5.60 tire has a larger rolling radius (10.9 inches vs. 11.2 inches), the tire revolutions per mile are reduced from 905 to 882. This represents a 2.5 percent reduction in tire revolutions per mile, which reduces engine speed for slight gains in fuel economy, engine life, and tire life. The speedometer is recalibrated to compensate for the slower turning tires."

The new tire, being slightly bigger, also increased the ride height and ground clearance by five/sixteenths, as Chakmakian noted.

The front seat had a new adjustment mechanism that provided for two inches greater seat travel, allowing more comfort for tall drivers. AMC even offered an accessory kit so that current owners could increase seat travel on existing cars.

The front seat cushion and back were redesigned for firmer support and comfort, and a new seat fabric was scheduled to go into production in late February of 1959. The new material was the same as used on the 1958 Deluxe and Super models of the Rambler American, Rambler 6 and Rebel V-8. Chakmakian described the fabric as having "a two-tone (black-gray) diamond pattern. For greater durability, the fabric is a 100 percent synthetic type which contains 30 percent nylon." The trim material for the seat bolster, door panels and rear seat area was also new. Trim code was changed from T600 to T971.

Weights were up a bit, an even 15 pounds, and the conscientious Chakmakian even provided the reader with a breakdown of where the extra weight came from:

Trunk Lid	3.45 lbs.
Vent Windows, both sides	5.40 lbs.
5.60 tires, five	6.15 lbs.
Total	15.00 lbs.

Beyond all the dry facts and figures, however, there was a red hot small car market that was growing by leaps and bounds. Demand for smaller cars was at a high level and the greatly enhanced Metropolitan was arriving just in time to take advantage of it. It must have seemed incredible, even to AMC's hopeful product planners; a mere five years earlier, the import and small car market in America was barely discernible but now it was the talk of the country. Most of the credit had to go to that tireless promoter of the smaller car, AMC Chairman George Romney. He had begun to preach the virtues of compact cars, and small cars, back in 1950 but for many years his words had fallen on deaf ears. But Romney was a persistent man, patient and persevering. Compact and small cars constituted an idea he believed in fully and passionately. He tenaciously continued his one-man crusade for sensible transportation and in the end his message was finally heard: Others joined the crusade and the American auto market began a sea change, as old ideas were gradually replaced by new ones.

A noticeable improvement in Met merchandising was the showroom sales catalog—it was now in vivid color. (From 1956 to 1958, the Met was displayed in a rather drab sales catalog.) The handsome new brochure, a collectible item today, presented a snappy illustration of two Metropolitans with their happy owners on the front cover. A young and handsome couple are shown with a yellow and white Met convertible, presumably ready to dash off to fun and adventure, while an obviously older couple, with a black and white Met hardtop, look on approvingly. "IMPORTED METROPOLITAN 1500" is the headline on the brochure cover, with the subtitle "Luxury in Miniature." Inside the brochure are illustrations that show

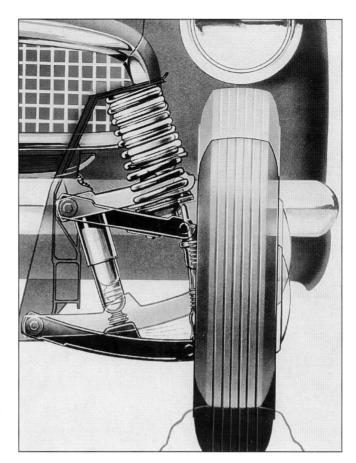

Details of Metropolitan's front suspension.

each of the color combinations offered, as well as what was becoming a famous quotation from *Popular Science Monthly's* Devon Francis, who had described the little Metropolitan as "A Watch-Charm Rolls-Royce."

Mets were popping up in the most unlikely places. The Columbus, Georgia, *Ledger-Enquirer* kept a fleet of 25 Met hardtops for its circulation department! All of the cars were black and white with the newspaper's insignia painted on the side of each. Circulation Manager E. E. Mullis was quoted as stating he was "well pleased with their performance and quality." The police department of Fairlawn, New Jersey, bragged about the town's right-hand drive Met patrol car, and the mayor had his picture taken at the wheel. Several companies even decided to have advertising messages printed on the vinyl spare tire cover, which was a clever yet inexpensive way to get publicity.

The motor press was still excited about the Met. *Economy Cars* had this to say: "the Metropolitan is saucy in styling and frisky as a kitten in performance." It liked the Met's power to weight ratio, saying "this amount of power comes close to thrusting the Metropolitan into the sports car class in performance." *Economy Cars* summed up its article by stating, "But its extra values, such as Continental styling, unitized construction, sports car-like handling and unusual performance, give it strong appeal for the young in heart of all ages."

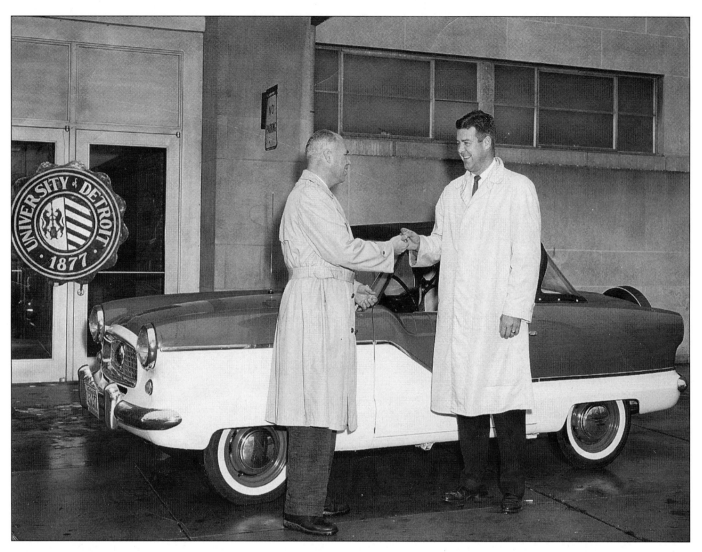

Bob Calihan, 6'4" tall basketball coach of the University of Detroit, takes delivery of his new Met from Ed Bailey of Bob's Rambler in Detroit.

Nor was *Economy Cars* alone. *Sports Car Illustrated* wrote a short report during 1959 that called the Metropolitan "Very aptly named," going on to say "the Metropolitan is a perfect car for dashing nimbly around the city, or for short trips along inter-urban expressways." It also noted: "The body is of unit-frame construction, and is quite solid and rattle free," and finished the piece by stating the combination of a short wheelbase and tight steering ratio "makes the Metropolitan a pleasure to park."

Jim Watson meanwhile was gathering up every colorful Met story or anecdote he could find and using them to keep the little car in the news. It was just about all he could do—his advertising budget was too small to flood the market with a mass message. In fact, Metropolitan ads are rather scarce, often consisting of only black and white quarter page pieces in family magazines. Many of the Met ads are reproduced throughout this book.

In 1959, the *Met Letter* carried photos of Met owners David Sawyer, described as a 6'6" tall star basket-ball player for the University of Pittsburgh, and Bob Calihan, a 6'4" basketball coach for the University of Detroit; so it was plain that the little Met had some pretty big fans—or at least tall ones.

Volkswagen was still the top-selling import. Its reputation as a reliable economy car of high quality was growing steadily. The French-built Renault was also growing in popularity, due more to low price and good marketing rather than any inherent goodness of the car. Many other imports were crowding the field, including such names as Vauxhall, Saab, Hillman, Opel, DKW, Citroen, Fiat, Panhard, Rover, Skoda, Sunbeam, and even the oddball German Goggomobil, all competing for a share of the burgeoning U.S. market. The Met was no longer a big fish in a small pond—the pond was growing rapidly.

American Motors published a new Data Book for the revised Met. The booklet, similar in design to earlier ones, highlighted the improvements. It also reached out a bit further in attempting to explain the uniqueness of the Met when it stated:

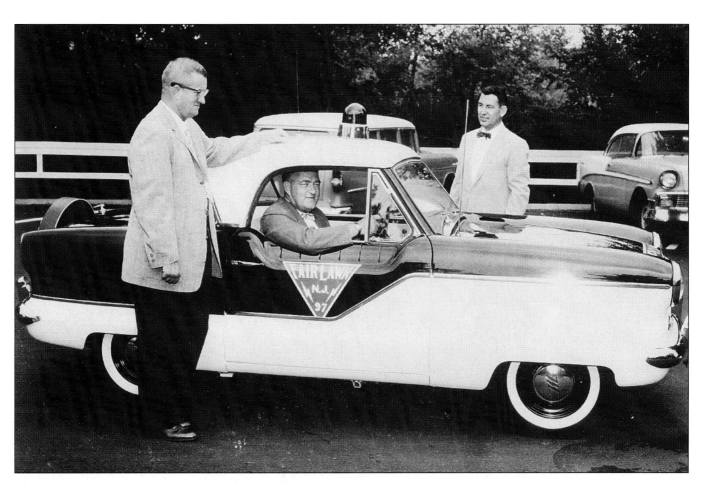

The Mayor of Fairlawn, New Jersey, Richard J. VanderPlaat tests the city's new Metropolitan police car in 1959.

Shown here are nineteen of the twenty-five Metropolitans used by the circulation department of the Ledge-Enquirer newspaper in Columbus, Georgia.

According to the 1959 press kit, the "deep-dip" rustproofing involved dipping the body in a tank of rustproofing primer paint as illustrated.

1959 Metropolitan convertible was a beauty from any angle.

Still pretty after all these years—1959 Met hardtop.

Mets being loaded for shipment to America, circa 1959.

"The Metropolitan is a different kind of a car representing a unique automotive concept created for the businessman confronted with today's frustrating traffic congestion, for the active homemaker who must daily perform countless errands, or for the young in heart who enjoy driving for the sheer fun of it."

The "bad" news for the Metropolitan was in the form of prior year sales figures for the Rambler American, figures that probably were still being pondered by Romney, sales boss Roy Abernethy and other AMC executives. It was a case of good news for the corporation being bad news for the Metropolitan. When finally totaled, sales in the prior year (the 1958 model year) showed a remarkable success for the reintroduced small Rambler, the 100 inch wheelbase American. Despite the limitations of offering only one body style (a two-door sedan that was really just a rework of the original 1950 Nash Rambler), the Rambler American hit a home run in the market. According to production records, a total of 29,375 of the 1958 models were produced. For the calendar year, which would include, of course, many early 1959 models, AMC reported that 42,196 Rambler Americans were registered.

Perhaps the only problem American Motors was experiencing with the Rambler American was that it couldn't build them fast enough to meet demand. It was becoming apparent that investments would soon have to be made for additional tooling and production equipment to take advantage of the soaring market. Sales of the American were, without a doubt, also eating into the Met's market, but it wasn't a big problem at this point. The improved Met was also having an exceptionally good year.

When considered with the undeniable advantage of hindsight, it appears that Romney himself was having some doubts about the long-term viability of his Metropolitan. In a speech titled "Today the New Car Buyer is Boss," he stated:

"In general, the American public is unwilling to accept some of the important disadvantages inherent in small foreign cars. Their useful space is somewhat too limited for the general American taste. Their noise level is high, their performance is less satisfactory...."

Romney was trying to make a point against imports vs. his own mainstream Rambler models, but it's doubtful he was unaware that he could also be referring to his own import. With AMC's comeback still in its infancy, every car sale was considered vital, so the Met's future was still safe. How long it would remain so was anyone's guess.

From the 1959 press kit—cutaway illustration of Met's sturdy unitized body construction.

Fashionable lady and her fashionable Metropolitan hardtop.

A somewhat obscure automotive magazine, *Foreign Cars Illustrated and Auto Sport*, road-tested a new Metropolitan for its July 1959 issue. Once it got beyond some snide remarks about the Met's appearance, it gave a generally positive review, stating: "Seat height from the floor is nine inches, so that you can relax without feeling cramped.... Seating three average sized adults in the front of the Metropolitan presents no great problem; I know, because we tried it." We wonder how long that writer's manuscript sat on the editor's desk, since the car they tested was not one of the revised Mets and therefore didn't have vent windows, an exterior trunk lid or any of the other improvements. However, the reporter did have some positive remarks to say about the rear seat, calling it: "Just the thing for children under 10.... The seven inches of knee room available with the front seat in the normal position is adequate for youngsters on a short trip, or on a longer jaunt punctuated by fairly frequent stops."

The Commander of the Traffic Bureau for the city of Burbank, California, also had some positive comments to make about the Met. Although normally used for parking patrol, Burbank's Metropolitan police car was ready for just about any kind of action. As Lt. Albert Stariha noted: "The fact that the car can carry two men makes it a regular patrol car. It is equipped with siren, red light, shotgun, and other equipment used on full-sized patrol units." Sounds like everyone's worst nightmare—a Met with an attitude.

While the idea of a Metropolitan police car might seem odd to us today, the Mets were, for the most part, chosen for light-duty service: parking patrol, meter reading and such. It was meant to be a comfortable, low-cost alternative to the vehicle that many communities frequently bought for such service—a three wheel motorcycle! At least one report claimed the Met also cost less than the motorcycle. Thus, the Met's ability to carry two passengers plus equipment and offer all-weather comfort at a low cost were clear advantages that any smart city manager could recognize.

American Motors earlier had added another good man to the sales team, and his influence on the Metropolitan was beginning to show more and more clearly. Guy Hadsall, the man in charge of Shows and Exhibits for American Motors, was a first-rate automobile marketer who had been hired by AMC in February of 1957. Hadsall's job with AMC was to plan and coordinate exhibits of the company's products. The job entailed arranging all the various aspects of displaying cars at the automobile shows throughout the country and he did his job with skill, competence and a bit of dash.

The year 1959 was a robust one for American Motors, with total dollar sales up 85 percent and net profit, after tax, more than double the previous year.

Collision: The Metropolitan, the Police Department and the Women's Movement.

Oh, for those lazy, crazy days before womens' liberation! Just take a glance at a suggestion put forth, in writing, by one police official, circa 1959:

"The ease with which the [Metropolitan] can handle parking patrol suggests that many police departments might find it feasible to use women in such cars as parking control officers. This would result in salary savings, and make it possible to assign male officers to police work which policewomen cannot do."

We're sure it must have seemed like a great idea back then to suggest the use of low-paid women to do the menial chores. Come to think of it, aren't we still fighting that battle?

Those Met police cars!

...and Around-Town Law Enforcement!

A number of law enforcement agencies are switching to the versatile, maneuverable two-man Metropolitan "1500" that provides low-cost operation combined with maximum protection. Durable Single-Unit construction assures extra safety in case of accident and the smart hardtop provides complete protection from the weather. A rear seat is handy for emergency equipment and the trunk can be opened from inside the car so that driver and passenger can get at contents quickly.

One demonstration ride in the versatile Met will convince officials in your town that this is an important step forward towards greater police efficiency!

The Metropolitan Is A *Better* Two-Man Police Vehicle

Versatile—The Metropolitan "1500" does everything a three-wheel motorcycle does for less money—plus helps in city speed control, other around-town duties.

Extra-Protection—Here's all-weather protection for around-the-clock police work—and Single-Unit construction means extra protection from traffic hazards.

Available with Right-Hand Drive—The Metropolitan "1500" is available with right-hand drive at no extra cost.

At the right, Captain Milton Odell, Assistant Chief of the Huntington Park, California, Police Department takes delivery of a Met to replace the former three-wheel motorcycle. Officials in your town, too, will find a Met the ideal police car.

Metropolitan "1500"

...more and more the 1st choice for law enforcement agencies!

This Met's owner fitted it with a wind-up key on the hood as a gag, repainted the body all white, except for door notches, which were painted black.

A Colorado doctor's wife sent AMC this photo of her 1959 Met hardtop with "Frosty" the dog perched on the front seat.

The 108 inch Ramblers were rapidly growing in sales and so was the smaller Rambler American. A new addition to the American lineup was a two-door station wagon, which helped fuel a dramatic increase in American deliveries.

The Metropolitan shared in all this success. In fact, 1959 ended up being the best year yet for sales of the petite auto. Shipments to America totaled 20,435, with an additional 1,774 shipped to Canada. Total U.S. and export wholesale sales to dealers were 16,956 for the fiscal year, according to the company's annual report (as recounted in the 1960 report). Calendar year retail sales in America were 14,959. That was certainly a worthy success, a solid sales performance for the little Met. The fact that it came from a product that was already on the market for six years makes it even more remarkable. What AMC didn't know, in fact what no one knew, was that 1959 was destined to be the climax, the peak, the best sales year the Met would ever have. The tiny Metropolitan had surged to its high water mark. That success proved beyond any doubt its inherent goodness and its undeniable appeal. Its staying power in the market, however, was still a question. Watson planned for even better sales in 1960.

The 1960 Metropolitan model year began on October 14, 1959. There were no substantive changes or

AMC's Manager of Shows & Exhibits, Guy Hadsall, came up with many clever Met displays.

John Harriman, financial columnist for the Boston Globe, with Metropolitan and Rambler American.

Handsome display of 1960 Mets at the Chicago Auto Show was typical of the careful attention to detail by AMC's Guy Hadsall.

Met advertisement has youthful, light-hearted flavor.

American Motors' Boston zone displayed these Mets in front of the zone office during Easter 1960.

Television actor and writer Johnny Clark sent in a little jingle to AMC that bragged "I'm a Metropolitan man!"

revisions to the car and none were to be expected since so many improvements had occurred during the prior model year. Pricing was up again, to $1,673 for the hardtop and $1,697 for the convertible. The Rambler American Deluxe two-door was now only about $100 more expensive than a Met hardtop, and to many people it probably appeared to be a much more substantial automobile. It didn't have the Met's engaging personality, of course, and it couldn't hope to match the Met's thriftiness with fuel. But it did hold five adults with a fair amount of comfort. Its

trunk was larger, its six-cylinder engine promised greater smoothness and power than the Met's Austin four, and its fuel economy was very good. The two cars even looked similar, with the Met appearing cuter and the American seeming larger and sturdier.

At least the convertible market was still wide open for the Met—the American series didn't offer a convertible. In the ragtop market, the Met was still priced competitively with other imports, and it had virtually no competition within AMC showrooms. In other words, if a prospect wanted an AMC convertible, then his choice was either to be shown a Metropolitan or be shown to the door.

Of course, imported (or "foreign" as many people termed them) cars were still only a small segment of the market. America in the 1960s was still somewhat distrustful of non-American products. "Made in the U.S.A." was a slogan that was steeped with pride—and with good reason. Many customers still preferred to "Buy American," often for patriotic reasons, sometimes for quality reasons. When those people decided to downsize to a smaller car, they invariably gravitated to the Rambler American or one of the new compacts offered by the Big Three: the Ford Falcon, Chevrolet Corvair and the Valiant from Chrysler Corporation. That was a part of the market the Met, and other imports, couldn't easily reach.

But the tide was turning towards the imports. Out in California, actor/songwriter Johnny Clark was an enthusiastic Met owner, writing to Jim Watson at AMC a letter that included a jingle about the joys of Met ownership (the last line of the lyric is "I'm a Met-

Pegge Saggus with her dad's Met convertible.

Everett Saggus of Georgia took this photo of his lovely daughter, Pegge, and what he called his "wonderful Met."

ropolitan Man!"). Meanwhile, down in Georgia, Everett Saggus, a photographer by trade, mounted a custom hood ornament, a small statue of a photographer, to his Met. He sent in photos of the car, shown with his lovely daughter, to Jim Watson. Saggus informed Watson that he used the Met to haul his speedboat to the water: ***"People around here laughed at me; said the little Met wouldn't pull the boat. Well, I showed 'em."*** Saggus added a postscript to his letter ***"P.S.: Yes, there is another car in my family. The wife has a 1958 Chevrolet, but it is seldom used since we got 'Mettized.'"***

Also from Georgia came a report of an airplane that stalled during an emergency landing near Buford and

Radio Station WKNB in Connecticut used Mets in its fleet.

landed on top of a Metropolitan hardtop. A photo of the incident appeared in the *Detroit Free Press*. Although the car sustained much sheet metal damage, all in all it survived its ordeal in surprisingly good shape. No injuries were reported by the occupants.

The Columbus, Ohio, *Star* newspaper gave the Met a rave when it headlined an article by Steve Bulkey **"Austin Mill Gives Met Missile-Like Take Off."** And Hartford, Connecticut, radio station WKNB, 840 on the dial, maintained a fleet of four Met hardtops. According to factory memos, the Met fleet had been leased from the big Rambler dealer in Hartford, Lippman Motors.

Most AMC dealerships had long since dropped their old Nash and Hudson signs, replacing them with new Rambler signs. Dealerships that carried both of the remaining AMC brands were called Rambler-Metropolitan dealers, in much the same way that Chrysler has Chrysler-Plymouth dealers and Ford has Lincoln-Mercury dealers. But it's probably at this point that people began to erroneously refer to the Met as the Rambler Metropolitan, dropping the hyphen and assuming that Rambler was the marque name and Metropolitan was the model. Several dealers even dropped the hyphen in their print advertising, which probably added to the confusion.

NO ONE WAS HURT when this light plane "conked out" while attempting an emergency landing near Buford, Ga., and came down atop this car carrying three persons.

From the Detroit Free Press, September 26, 1960.

More Mets from Radio Station WKNB, Hartford, Connecticut.

1960 Met advertisement. Note prominent Rambler-Metropolitan letters at bottom of ad, probably one reason why many people still refer to the Met as a Rambler, which it wasn't.

This Pennsylvania man wrote to AMC, "I like the American Motors quality—my next family car will be a Rambler."

Pennsylvania family with Metropolitan.

Down in sunny Florida, a star ballerina of the world famous Cypress Gardens Water Ski Show, Nancy Legant, was the proud and happy owner of a yellow and white Met convertible. According to a letter from the Cypress Gardens public relations manager: *"I think the car and Nancy capture the spirit and feeling of the young American outdoor girl. The car and Nancy compliment [sic] each other."*

A Pennsylvania man expressed his satisfaction with his Met in a letter he sent to AMC in mid-1960.

"Gentlemen!" he wrote, **"A few months ago when I purchased a Metropolitan I had no intention to join the club because I could not see any reason to do so. I know different now. I purchased the Metropolitan in addition to a Buick for only one reason, economize transportation for short trips. I found something else; driving pleasure, which I did not experience in my other car in spite of automatic shift, power equipment, electric windows, seats, etc. My wife as well as my oldest son prefer**

Cypress Gardens photo of star water ski ballerina, Nancy Legant, her Met convertible, and other Cypress Gardens water skiers enjoying the Florida sunshine. (Photo courtesy of Cypress Gardens)

Nancy Legant, her Met, and lovely Florida scenery in Cypress Gardens. (Photo courtesy of Cypress Gardens)

LADIES' DAYS ... AT BAIR MOTORS, INC.

ATTENTION:

Housewives, Secretaries, Nurses, School Teachers, Sales Ladies, Students, Waitresses, Etc.

Did you know that there is one car that will fill all your motoring needs, regardless of whether it's a daily round trip to work, or just to the corner grocery?

- ✓ It's Fun to Own !
- ✓ Kitten Smooth in Traffic !
- ✓ It's Personal as Your Powder Puff !
- ✓ It Operates Out of A Change Purse !
- ✓ Very Smart and Fashionable !
- ✓ It's Fun to Drive !

UP TO 35 MILES PER GAL.

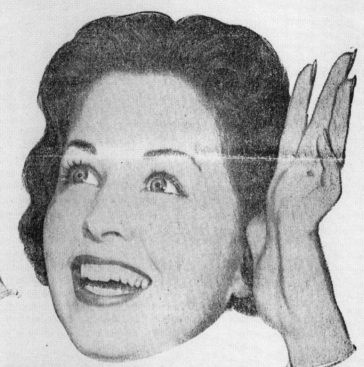

And, A Brand New One Costs Less Than A Late Model Used Car!

THIS WEEK IS "MET" WEEK!

Ladies, Now You Can Buy A Beautiful New Metropolitan Hardtop for As Little As...

$1795

OR, BUY A CONVERTIBLE FOR ONLY $25 MORE !

AND You Get...
ABSOLUTELY FREE:

Beautiful Tutone Paint
Radio and Heater
Smart White Sidewall Tires
36,000 Mile Warranty
Free Lubrication For One Year

PLUS: We Buy Your Gasoline For the First 2,500 Miles of Driving !

All Yours for $100, Plus Tax and License Down!

MONTHLY PAYMENTS OF JUST $55.88

BANK RATE FINANCING !
Down Payment Is No Problem !

BAIR MOTORS, INC.

NOW OPEN SUNDAYS
For Your Shopping Convenience !

362 WEST GRANT at HIGHWAY 395   —   PHONE SH 5-7341

Bair Motors ran this eye-catching advertisement for a Met hardtop for $1,795, or a convertible for only $25 more.

the Metropolitan for their errands. There is something special between owners of this fine car. Even my youngest son (age four) knows if he is the first one to spot another Metropolitan, he waves to the driver. He always gets a friendly response."

Oh yes, this owner added a postscript to his handwritten letter. *"P.S.: I like the American Motors quality. My next family car will be a Rambler."*

American Motors produced a wonderful piece of sales literature for the Metropolitan that year. It's delightful in the way it expresses the Met's appeal and the reasons for desiring one in terms that nowadays would make a feminist blanch. And yet, who sincerely can find fault with the simple ideals expressed herein:

CAREER GIRLS KNOW ... IT'S THE METROPOLITAN "1500," The Personal Car for Girls on the Go!

Railroad man S. E. Bellgraph rigged a special carrier on his Met.

Go ahead—lose your heart over this smart little, chic little car. It's the most wonderful way in the world to go! Magic-carpets you through heavy traffic in minutes, on pennies! You'll love the jet-smooth ride of the Met, an American kind of ride you're used to. Plenty of room for you and him and packages or pets. The sit-up-and-notice performance leaves you slightly breathless and pleasantly surprised. Ideal for cross-country cruises. A product of American Motors, at your Rambler-Metropolitan dealer.

One magazine noted, during 1960, that *"the Metro still looks like a scaled-down Nash of years ago. Surprising many people, the Metro has somehow managed to hang onto an amazing share of the import market."*

Although the Met's appeal was still strong, the market for two-seat automobiles simply wasn't growing at anything approaching the rate of demand for four-passenger sedans. The undeniable utility of a family economy compact outweighed the appeal of spunky styling and fancy appointments. And even the Met's styling was becoming a little bit old hat. After all, it was now four years since its last freshening. The Met's enclosed wheels harkened back to the Airflyte days of Nash, and Nash of course was now just a memory. Even the big Nash had ceased featuring enclosed front wheels in its final year of production, 1957. Although demand for the Met was brisk, it was starting to tail off. According to the American Motors Annual Report for 1960, wholesale sales of Mets to dealers, U.S. and export, totaled 13,459 vs. the 16,956 reported for fiscal 1959. (AMC's fiscal year at the time ran from October to September.) That was a drop of 20.62 percent. In that same time frame, however, Rambler sales increased 25.8 percent to a whopping 464,790. Basically, the same dealers were selling both lines, so it had little to do with the dealer network but a great deal to do with basic demand for the car. That fact did not go unnoticed by AMC's management.

A series of recently discovered memos sheds a little more light on the problem. American Motors vehicle distribution department sent a monthly report on Metropolitan sales to the British Consulate in Detroit, Michigan. The reports list retail sales of Metropolitans in the U.S., Canada, Export Markets (Mets were sold in Africa and several European countries) and the U.K. Each report gives sales figures for the preceding month, as well as a cumulative total of all Met sales. Many of the months are missing, but what has turned up thus far shows a definite trend; as 1960 wore on, Met retail sales steadily dropped, instead of showing the large increase that Watson had planned for. Inventories of unsold Mets began to soar.

Jim Watson didn't lose his enthusiasm for the Metropolitan and, in fact, was ready with a surprise this year. The Spring 1960 issue of the *Met Letter* gave some details of what it would be. "SPECIAL MET MADE FOR THE N.Y. SHOW," it stated. "For the very

Lyrical booklet advised girls to "lose your heart over this smart little, chic little car."

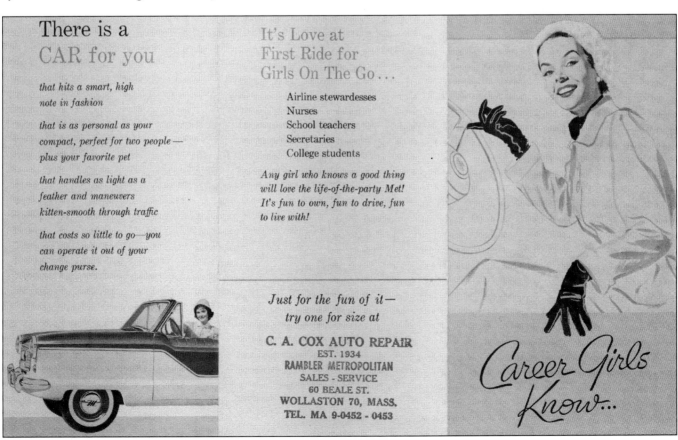

Slightly sexist prose was appropriate for the time, 1960.

This little girl's mother was the proud owner of a Met hardtop.

Vacation time in a Met.

Mob scene at the auto show when the Metropolitan Fifth Avenue was on display. Note young woman at center, wearing bunny ears. Note also "World's Smartest Smaller Car" slogan, and young girls wearing paper Volkswagen hats at left.

first time, a special Met has been built for a special automobile show ... the International Auto Show scheduled for April 16-24 in New York's Coliseum." The auto show special was called the "Fifth Avenue" and it was a stunningly beautiful car. Painted in Pearlescent Easter Parade Pink, all one color rather than with contrasting white paint, it looked, of course, like a giant Easter egg. The upholstery was special, too, with pink top grain leather used. Rugs were thick pink plush (like shag) and the door notch was finished in white Pearlescent leather.

It was a sensation at the New York Auto Show. Guy Hadsall outdid himself in preparing the promotion. Pretty girls wearing bunny ears accompanied the car on a special rotating display stand that was covered with the same pink carpeting as in the show car. Drawings were held on a regular basis, seven times each day of the show, for the chance to win either a 32-inch "cuddle bunny" or a 42 inch "Harvey bunny." Thirty-five of the smaller size stuffed bunnies and seven of the larger were awarded every day. One of the rules was that winners had to be in attendance

This lucky lady, Dorothy Gillis, won a new Met during a Los Angeles Met promotion.

Newscaster George Putnam draws the winning ticket in a "Win A Free Metropolitan" promotion.

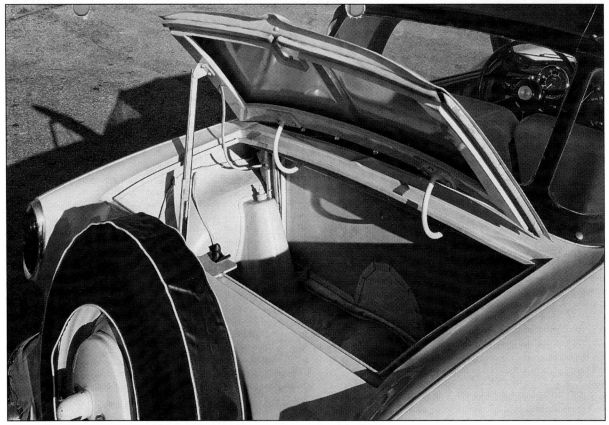

Attempts were made to offer a kit so owners of pre-1959 Mets could retrofit outside trunk lids but these proved too complex and costly. Note (top photo) the lid still has the raised metal bead that was eliminated on production cars when lids were introduced. (Bottom photo) Retrofit lid in raised position.

when the lucky numbers were drawn, so the Metropolitan stand, naturally, ended up being crowded with onlookers most of the day, seeming to be the hottest display in the show.

The response to the Metropolitan Fifth Avenue was outstanding, with the little jewel of a car winning wide acclaim. Spurred on by the reaction, more special Mets were soon planned. These are covered in more detail in Chapter Six.

Also in 1960, Watson's *Met Letter*, which went out to all members of the Metropolitan Club, was advertising a line of Met jewelry that included a money clip, key chain, charm bracelet, set of cuff links (remember cuff links?) and tie clasp, ladies brooch and other items. Also, from Hubley Co. of Lancaster, Pennsylvania, came 1/24th scale Met promotional toy cars. The Hubley promos, beautifully detailed and produced in authentic colors, are considered desirable and collectible today.

In an ominous preview of the unfair trade practices that would become rampant in later decades, AMC's director of automotive exports, W. H. Thoreson spoke out against "discriminatory practices" involving U.S. cars shipped to Europe. "Not only are duty and taxes in European countries set at almost prohibitive lev-

Two happy motorists and a Met hardtop.

els" he was quoted as saying "but shipping charges from East Coast ports to Europe are double those for the same car coming back to the U.S." This wasn't a case of a businessman crying sour grapes, however; exports of his popular Ramblers were up. The point he was trying to make was that inequitable trade practices should be stopped before they got out of

Detroit advertising executive W. David Kludt traded in his Cadillac on a Met. "It's great!" he said.

1960 Met at Springfield, Massachusetts, Auto Show.

hand. Looking back on how American products were effectively locked out of many foreign markets during the past two decades, it's a shame no one bothered to pay attention to his warning.

AMC ended the Metropolitan's 1960 model year on October 11, 1960. Retail sales were down, wholesale shipments were down, inventory was piling up and the outlook for the future was beginning to get hazy. This was the tail end of the first year of a new decade, and stylewise the Metropolitan was starting to get a bit long in the tooth. There were many new competitors in the market now: low priced, roomy compacts from many foreign countries, all vying for the same thing the Met needed—the new car buyer. But the biggest competitor the Met now faced was the one that showed up just across the showroom floor. For 1961, American Motors decided to field a restyled Rambler American and it was a honey.

Chapter Five

The End of the Line (1961-1962)

October 12, 1960, was pegged as the official starting date for the Metropolitan's 1961 model year. As was true a few times already in the past, the introduction date itself was the most significant indicator of the new Met—the cars themselves were virtually identical to the previous model year.

What was new in AMC showrooms this year was a completely reskinned Rambler American. AMC Styling Director Edmund Anderson and his staff revised the sheet metal of the existing 100-inch wheelbase American, coming up with styling that made the car both more compact than before and all-new in appearance. The American line consisted of two- and four-door sedans and a two-door station wagon, as it had in 1960, and also added a new four-door station wagon and a convertible to the series. Tooling costs were well below what might ordinarily be expected since the changes were only skin deep. The basic chassis and inner body stampings of the previous American were retained. The tooling for these items

had long since been amortized and because of that AMC was able to keep American prices at rock bottom levels. The prior American had proven to be a real competitor in the showroom, and now with new styling, plus the addition of a handsome new convertible, it could be expected to draw even more sales away from the Met. The Met convertible was still priced considerably lower than the American convertible ($1,697 for the Met vs. $2,369 for the American), but the latter had the advantage of being a six-passenger car and could be had with power steering, power brakes, automatic transmission, air conditioning and a whole slew of other options that were simply unavailable on Metropolitans.

The reasons why AMC chose to allocate its scant product development funds to the American, rather than the Metropolitan, can be stated rather simply. Arguments put forth in favor of the American were that it appealed to a broader share of the market, since it held more passengers, and also that it was a

The 1961 Metropolitans.

This lovely young woman proudly displays the 1961 Met hardtop.

The owners of this Met had an Ambassador and Rambler Classic in their garage plus this cute Met convertible in the driveway.

larger, more "market acceptable" size. It's probable, too, that the profit margin on Americans was higher than that on Metropolitans. Another important consideration was that with the American, AMC earned a manufacturing profit as well as a sales profit.

Earlier discussions among product planners, circa 1956 and 1957, had centered on redesigning the Met as a four-passenger car. Paradoxically, the Met would probably need to be built on a longer wheelbase if it was going to become a full four-passenger car and thus attract a larger market share. But that meant it would have to be completely redesigned, which would squeeze its profit margin. Yet, if it was merely reskinned (like the American eventually was) it probably wouldn't realize a substantial increase in sales, because the market for two seater automobiles simply wasn't large enough. AMC also considered offering a four-passenger Met station wagon built on the existing chassis. But the product planners felt it was unlikely that such a vehicle would ever sell as much volume or be as profitable as a reintroduced Rambler American. One AMC market analyst figured a wagon would increase Met sales only about 25 percent because the number of hardtop Mets would decline when shoppers chose the wagon instead. The analyst estimated the total number of Met sales possible with a three model lineup (hardtop, convertible and wagon) at 24,500 units per year. That was not enough to justify setting up a new assembly line in America nor even retooling the British plant. Interestingly, when calculating these numbers AMC figured on selling the wagon for the same price as the hardtop.

Another consideration was the increasing competition, both within the showroom from the American and outside, from other imported cars. The import automobile market was then experiencing rapid growth. The Met's share of the market, expressed as a percentage, continued to decrease, hit by the double whammy of a market that was growing larger while Met unit sales grew smaller. Meanwhile, the Rambler was making news every day as a sales phenomenon, and it's easy to imagine that Rambler salesmen were more inclined to concentrate their efforts on their hottest products.

That wasn't the case for imaginative dealers in a few select markets. A good example was in Compton, California, where the local Metropolitan dealer, Friendly Rambler, decided to do something unique to help merchandise his Metropolitans. General Manager and owner Jim Fisk decided the best way to spur sales was to have his dealership offer custom features on Mets to increase their desirability. A typical ad read: **"ONLY AT FRIENDLY IS YOUR METROPOLITAN COMPLETELY CUSTOMIZED TO YOUR INDIVIDUAL TASTE AT NO EXTRA COST!"**

What Fisk offered his customers was luxurious interior upholstery and trim, plus fancy deep-pile carpeting. Certain custom touches, such as a metal spare tire cover, chromed tailpipe extension, gas cap

An Ohio family and their 1960 Met hardtop.

and window moldings, etc., were added according to the customer's desire. Fancy full wheel covers were available, as were dual side view mirrors. If the customer so wished, the exterior could also be treated to a repaint in exclusive colors that were not available from the factory, including single tone (monotone) paint. The owner of Friendly Rambler gave the custom cars a name he felt was worthy of their special status; he called them the "Jim Fisk Specials."

Okay, so Mr. Fisk wasn't exactly modest in choosing a model name. Regardless, his custom Mets were distinctive autos. Only a few photos of the Fisk Mets have surfaced thus far and we've included them here. Are these cars rare? Well, as Friendly Rambler noted in its advertisements: **"THERE IS NO 'JIM FISK SPECIAL' ANYWHERE ELSE IN THE COUNTRY. SEE THEM EXCLUSIVELY AT … FRIENDLY RAMBLER!"**

When AMC's Los Angeles Zone Manager R. M. Stevenson reported to Watson in October of 1961 the details of Fisk's program, he noted that Friendly's sales manager told him that the interior changes generated more interest and sales than the exterior work. When the dealership first began the program, they had simply repainted the exterior of the cars and that didn't seem to attract much attention. But as soon as they began to put the emphasis on interior customizing, with tuck and roll seat upholstery, plush carpeting and nicer side panels, sales took off! Stephenson wrote "this has changed the minds of the sales force as to the salability of Metros and they are making as good, or better, commissions then [sic] on regular Ramblers…. The percentage of these customized Metropolitans sold to regular Metros sold is about one-third or 30 percent…. The outstanding feature of this program is that it appeals to the women." Fisk evidently agreed with that assessment. A local paper quoted him as saying, "Never underestimate the power of a woman and the appeal of tuck and roll naugahyde upholstery."

That same year a different dealer contacted Jim Watson with an urgent request—the sale of a Met hinged on being able to obtain an air conditioning

Advertisement for Friendly Rambler, home of the "Jim Fisk Special" Metropolitans.

unit that would fit the car. Watson scouted around, finally sending back a Teletype saying that a company in Dallas, Texas, offered an air conditioning kit for the Met, priced at just $222 wholesale. Oddly, it doesn't seem that anyone at AMC pursued the idea of offering the kit through Met dealers.

Metropolitan factory advertisements continued their understated approach, though the message was, as usual, slanted to singles. "Metropolitan is meant for you if ... you desire smart, sensible, personal transportation at more reasonable costs ..." read one print advertisement.

Met sales fell again in 1961. The American Motors annual report for that fiscal year listed wholesale sales, U.S. and export of 8,142, a drop of 39.5 percent. The report also listed U.S. retail sales for the fiscal year of 9,130, still a 32.6 percent decline. Sales of Ramblers were also down, but even so, they were outselling Mets by a ratio of 41:1. The Met's share of the import market dropped, too. Watson reported the Met's share, based on registrations January through

October of 1961, was only 2.4 percent. In the Minneapolis Zone, the Met's share was an even lower 1.1 percent. Things looked dismal.

It looked about the same for retail sales for the calendar year. The 12 months of 1961 showed 8,881 Mets were sold at retail, according to Watson. In fact, almost every zone, in every part of the country, failed to reach its sales quota. Only the Los Angeles zone exceeded its goal, selling 128.53 percent of plan. But unfortunately, that was an isolated case. For the most part, sales in California were as tough to make as everywhere else, as witnessed by the San Francisco zone, which reached only 58.1 percent of its quota. The saddest part of all this was these were modest objectives and yet still couldn't be attained.

But, conversely, that doom and gloom wasn't universal. Of the top 10 Metropolitan dealers in America for 1961, most had actually reported sales increases. Coon Bros., in Detroit, saw a small 7.4 percent increase, while Hardy Motor Company in Mobile, Alabama, was up 42.2 percent. Central Florida Rambler-

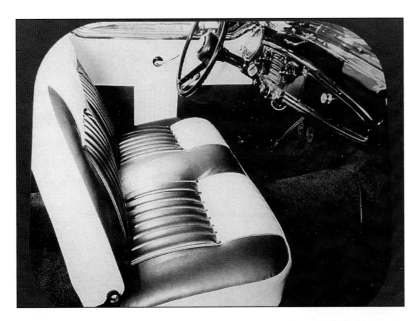

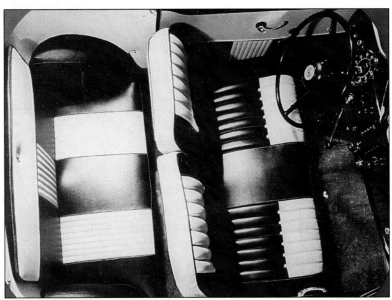

Interiors were opulent in the "Jim Fisk Special" Mets.

Jim Fisk's Friendly Rambler was at one point the top-selling Metropolitan dealer in the country.

Custom spare tire cover was an aftermarket option.

Metropolitan, in Winter Haven, managed to hammer out a whopping 275 percent increase in Met sales! For 1961, the top volume Metropolitan dealer in America was Jim Fisk's Friendly Rambler, where the combination of good service and customized Mets pushed it to a 162.8 percent Met sales increase.

Jim Watson, optimist that he was, read good news into all these numbers. In a sales talk to dealers Watson noted, "It is significant that nine of the ten leading dealers in 1961 exceeded their 1960 sales." It seemed to prove that success was attainable to those who would put the proper effort into the job. He suggested that other dealers should follow Fisk's example.

Watson certainly was correct as far as percentages go, but the raw unit sales numbers, which he showed the dealers, clearly pointed out one large problem; although those nine dealers had indeed increased their sales, the unit numbers were still tiny when compared to sales of Ramblers. Coon Bros., for instance, managed to sell just 58 Mets during 1961,

METROPOLITAN
is meant for you
if...

- You desire smart, sensible, *personal* transportation at more reasonable costs.

- You appreciate "Luxury in Miniature."

- You like sparkling, yet thrifty power and performance in town *and* country.

- You enjoy unusual handling ease in traffic and in parking.

- You seek the safety and quietness of Single-Unit construction . . . the long car life resulting from Deep-Dip rustproofing.

Choose from Hardtop Coupe or smart Convertible models.

AMERICAN MOTORS'
Metropolitan 1500
"THE ROYAL RUNABOUT"

SEE YOUR RAMBLER-METROPOLITAN DEALER

"Metropolitan is meant for you..." reads this 1961 Met advertisement.

Although her Met has the outside trunk lid, this lady's husband built a small trailer to haul their luggage for a trip from Ohio to Florida. Note "Crosley" hubcap on trailer's wheel.

Central Florida Metropolitan sold 60, and the Hardy Motor Company sold a less than hearty 91 units for the year. Friendly Rambler, which, being the highest volume Met agency for 1961, was the top dog, the *numero uno*, had retailed just 113 Mets for the year. Compared to the Rambler's tremendous sales, these numbers must have seemed insignificant to dealers and probably also to many of the top executives at AMC.

Nor were things getting any better. AMC's factory-owned inventory of new, unsold Metropolitans was fairly high. Watson pointed this out during the same sales meeting. His slide projector showed a chart that listed Met inventory using the standard way it's figured in the automobile business even today—by day's supply. Watson's chart showed that AMC had 893 Mets in stock as of December 15, 1961. That doesn't seem like an overly large number but then again it didn't include Met inventory that was already parked on dealers' lots. Still, what those 893 Mets represented was about a 98-day supply for AMC and that was simply too much inventory. This was especially true in the St. Louis zone, where the day's supply of Mets was officially listed by Watson as "*Ad Infinitum.*"

Not only was it too much inventory, but at many of the zone offices it was also lopsided regarding color choices. Looking at the 14 larger factory zone warehouses, the total number of Mets in stock was 724 units. Of those cars, 490 were of the yellow/white paint combination. That meant that overall, 67.6 percent of the new Metropolitans in factory zone inventory were yellow. That was the average, so obviously some zones were stuck with an even higher percentage of yellow cars in stock. Some of the inventory numbers have survived over the years and they graphically point out the problem areas. The Detroit zone inventory was the most perfectly unbalanced; exactly 100 percent of Mets in stock were the yellow and white combination. That certainly would limit a

Lovely young lady and her Metropolitan hardtop.

dealer's choice. It also would cost AMC some retail sales since, if a dealer didn't happen to have a customer's preferred color in stock, he couldn't readily purchase a suitable car from zone stock for resale to the customer. Unless, of course, the customer wanted a yellow car. Henry Ford, who had once offered his cars in "any color, so long as it's black" must have smiled in his grave.

Watson came up with an idea that he felt would help the situation. Sometime earlier, when the Los Angeles zone was stuck with too many black and white Mets in stock, Watson had ordered the construction of a custom Metropolitan called the Royal Runabout. It was an all-black Met hardtop with special interior and trim. The Royal Runabout was displayed at auto shows and selected dealerships to help generate interest in the regular black and white Mets. It did the trick, creating demand that cleared out the old inventory so well that an extra supply had to be brought in to satisfy orders. Watson now planned to use the same approach to solve his yellow car problem. He ordered the building of another Royal Runabout hardtop, this one to be painted a rich pearlescent yellow. Although the car wouldn't be the same shade of yellow as the production autos and would be monotone rather than two-tone, Watson believed it would create enough excitement to sell out the bloated inventory.

In retrospect, Watson's suggestion that other dealers follow the example set by Friendly Rambler doesn't seem like a realistic solution to the sales problem. What Fisk was doing took quite a bit of time and labor—and also involved finding companies with the skill to fabricate and install custom interior trim, and other companies that could offer a quality repaint job at a reasonable price. Those sorts of services might be readily available in a car-crazy culture like California, but could a small dealer in, say, Nebraska really expect to find those talents within his own community? Furthermore, many dealers simply didn't want to be bothered working that hard for those few extra sales. Repaint the cars? Change the interiors? After all, Ramblers were selling like the proverbial hot cakes, with considerably less effort.

Time doesn't stand still, especially in the automobile business. October of 1961 came around and with it the opening of the 1962 Metropolitan model year. Announcement day was set for the 6th of the month and again the date was the most significant thing about the new model year. There were no notable changes to the Metropolitan and as a matter of fact, there were still so many Mets in stock that few new cars had to be shipped over. Dealers could sell from the shelves, so to speak. As in all prior model changeovers, any unsold Mets still in stock as of the new model announcement date were simply sold and titled as current year cars—no leftovers!

The Metropolitan's color brochure was updated and reprinted again. The cover still showed the same

The Met brochure for 1962 was, like the cars themselves, nearly identical to the 1959 issue.

two Mets, a black and white hardtop and a yellow and white convertible, along with the same two couples. In fact, probably the easiest way to tell the 1962 brochure from the 1959 issue is to look at the date on the back cover of each.

Sales were stuck in low gear and it was becoming increasingly obvious to many that the Met's days were numbered. Dealer interest, for the most part, was lacking and the public itself had moved on to other imported cars—particularly the VW Beetle. By this time, the Beetle's design was so far out-of-date that it seemed almost to be coming back in style, at least among people who wanted to make an anti-Detroit fashion statement. The Beetle was small, economical, well built, reliable and could seat four people. With the exception of that last qualifier, the exact same things could be said of the Metropolitan. And there's the rub. Success might hinge on only one thing, but unfortunately it was an insurmountable thing. The poor little Met was nearing the end of the road.

Jim Watson hadn't given up, however. He'd spent most of his life in automobile sales, and it's quite like-

An Ohio pharmacy had the Easter Bunny drive through town in a Met to promote sales of Easter candy.

Press photographers Mike Blizzard and Glen Gorman gave high marks to Met's durability, and used spare tire covers for free advertising. Shown are a 1961 hardtop and 1959 convertible.

The Reverend Clifford Brier wrote: "People here are well aware that the Metropolitan zipping by means that this Priest is busily making calls…"

Bernice Gilmore of Ohio stated, "I have never had a sweeter nor better performing car."

ly he understood the Met's precarious position in the company lineup. But Watson seems to have decided that, if indeed the Met's time was nearly over, at least it would go down swinging. He reminded his dealers of the Met's intended position: "As we have said many times, the Met is in our line to broaden our market coverage and to enable us to better meet the varied automotive transportation needs of our customers," he said. He further stated, "That it has a strong appeal to and well meets the needs of certain motorists continues to be proved by the flow of unsolicited owner letters received." He read from a letter sent in by a photographer for the *Atlantic City Press*. The cameraman wrote: "I can't see how a Met stays together with the rough treatment we give them. There are now more and more people using Mets for business and pleasure because of stability, room, riding pleasure and economy."

There was letter from the Reverend Brier of Illinois who wrote: "I am now the proud and delighted owner of a Met which exceeds all my expectations. I wouldn't trade it for a Cadillac. In appearance, performance and comfort, it is in a class by itself.... Just the other week I gave four nuns a ride in it—all at once, veils and everything—and they were amazed at its roominess. People here are well aware that the Metropolitan zipping by means that this priest is busily making calls and I unhesitatingly brag about and recommend this car to all. Recently I drove 300 miles one morning in my Met and was more than delighted with its performance and comfort on this trip. It was more of a joy than ever."

In January Watson advised his dealers to keep pushing their inventory. ***"We all know that fast turnover is one of the prime objectives of good business management. We have long been striving to work our heavy Met inventories down to a 30 day's supply.... With the extension of the special merchandising allowance through March 31st,*** *we should soon be able to reach our 30 day turnover objective. Once there, the supply demand situation should never be permitted to get out of hand again."*

Heaven knows he tried to find new ways to draw attention to the struggling Met. "It is interesting to note that, as many of you are aware, the new National League baseball team in New York has been named the Metropolitans and for short will be known as the New York Mets with Casey Stengel as manager. This certainly is a publicity windfall for you boys in the immediate New York area...."

Watson continued to push for sales but it was a losing battle. In March he wrote a letter to regional and zone managers spelling out the results of the latest sales campaign, called "Break-Thru '62." Only one zone was running ahead of its quota, and most of the

This Kingston, New York, woman loved her Met convertible; her 13-year-old son could hardly wait to get his driver's license so he could drive it, too.

rest were far behind. What was most disappointing was the overall Met sales objective for the first quarter—total U.S. sales of 1,800 units. Watson noted: "With several zones with practically no Mets in stock anywhere, what happens this last ten days of March depends a great deal on whether the boats arrive in time to make it physically possible to get these badly needed cars delivered by midnight, Saturday the 31st. We certainly hope they make it. In the meantime we need all the help possible from those of you whose dealers have cars on hand ready for delivery now. Let's wind up this Break-Thru '62 Campaign with a big bell-ringing-Met ten days, too." He signed the letter "Yours for making the most of what you have, J. W. Watson."

In April, when James Watson wrote the final report on the first quarter sales promotion, he had to admit that the modest goal of 1,800 sales in three months had not been attained. Instead, the dealers were able to retail just 1,377 Mets. Only the Atlanta zone was able to beat its quota, selling 90 Mets vs. a goal of 87. The hoped-for boat load of Mets evidently didn't arrive in time. Watson wrote: "We are sure a number of you could have turned in better performance had you received cars in time, which unfortunately you did not. However, these new shipments should be in early enough this month to enable you to step up your

Met convertible is a stylish little machine indeed.

volume substantially. It is important that we continue to move these Mets out at retail. So keep gnawing away on 'em."

The Metropolitan's time had clearly passed, so it shouldn't have come as a shock when American Motors announced, on the 23rd of that same month, that it was phasing out its little import. Nevertheless, the news must have felt like a kick in the stomach to the

The Westbury, New York, woman who owned this black and white hardtop dubbed it the "Lil Shopping Bag."

thousands of loyal Met owners. The news release itself was rather terse:

STATEMENT CONCERNING METROPOLITAN

Our contract with British Motors for the production of Metropolitan automobiles has been completed.

When we introduced the car in 1954, we announced that we did so on a market-testing basis, while placing our primary emphasis on the focal center of the changing automobile market with the Rambler.

The growth segment of the market has proved to center around the Rambler concept, with this type of car now accounting for 37 percent of total U.S. car sales.

It does not appear to us that the present market is substantial for cars of the two-passenger Metropolitan size, since most Americans prefer family-sized automobiles. Nevertheless, we are continuing our research and exploration in the small car field.

Our national inventory of Metropolitans is below 1,000 and we expect our dealers to move them readily. Replacement parts are stocked right along with Rambler parts in this country, and our Rambler-Metropolitan dealers will provide continuing service for the thousands of Metropolitan owners.

It appears this pretty lady had a fondness for small dogs and small cars.

Sales Vice-President Thomas A. Coupe added a bit more explanation in a letter he sent to dealers. It read: "Recent developments in the industry confirm the general belief that the market for a smaller type vehicle is expected to be somewhat limited in this country. This is more significantly true of a two-passenger specialized vehicle such as the Metropolitan. Undoubtedly the growth segment of the market is in

This Hartsdale, New York, owner of a black and white Met hardtop wrote: "I actually feel safer in my little Met than I do in our other car."

the Rambler size cars which are now accounting for 37 percent of the market."

The task of actually notifying British Motors (the combine that Austin was now part of) that AMC was cancelling the Met program went to Roy D. Chapin, Jr., son of one of the founders of Hudson. Chapin joined AMC when Hudson merged with Nash and he enjoyed a notable career, later becoming chairman of the board. But in 1962 he was in charge of international sales for AMC and the Metropolitan program was considered part of that. Chapin recalled, some years afterwards, "It had been decided to end the Metropolitan and concentrate on the (Rambler) American, as that way we could earn a manufacturing profit as well as a sales profit, which would be more than the distributor profit we were making on the Met."

So it ended. Total inventory of unsold Metropolitans was less than a thousand units and dealers were given a $200 merchandising allowance to help clear them out.

One of Watson's last acts as Metropolitan Sales Manager was to write to his beloved Met Club members telling them the heartbreaking news about the car whose joyfulness they had shared. He held out hope, writing: "Your attention is directed to this statement in the [press] release. *'Nevertheless we are continuing our research and exploration in the small car field.'*

"When and if we have anything to report in this connection you will be advised."

Evidently, Watson still believed there might be a replacement for the Met someday in the future. In the meantime he advised Met Club members that other AMC cars might suit their needs. "The 100 inch wheelbase Rambler American is the next size in our American Motors line and we recommend it to you highly."

Actually, AMC's head of design, Edmund Anderson, sometime earlier had prepared a work flow chart for his studios that indicated a work schedule for what he called a Metropolitan "Y" to be ready for 1963/64. But the chart was from an earlier year and no formal program had ever developed. And anyway, Anderson was gone now, retired in Mexico.

Watson also believed, even as late as May, that the Met Club would be continued, and he advised members they could expect to see the Summer 1962 issue of the *Met Letter* soon. That didn't happen. Someone higher up killed the club and its letter. Floyd Clymer, who had test driven a Met hardtop up Pikes Peak back in the good old days, ended up reviving the club. Watson sent him a list of Met Club members that were still considered active at the end of production. It totaled just shy of 20,000 members. Clymer kept the club going a while but in the end it, too, was discontinued.

Seventy-eight-year-old retiree Nathan Townley took a motor trip to Florida in his Met, which he named "Little Joe."

George Romney left the company to pursue a career in politics, and the board of directors elected Roy Abernethy as president of the company. Once released from the constraints of what he called the "Romney Image," Abernethy chose to redirect AMC's efforts on larger and flashier cars; and that meant the Met had no hope of revival at AMC.

Later that same year, a New York dealer contacted Watson, supposedly at the request of Franklin D. Roosevelt Jr., who was a Fiat distributor and Jaguar dealer headquartered in Washington, D.C. According to a letter in Watson's files, the dealer claimed to have "talked with Roosevelt about the possibility of building the present Metropolitan in one of the common market countries for distribution throughout the world including the United States." Watson passed the information on to Abernethy, but the big boss had no interest in selling the Metropolitan's tooling.

By July of 1962, Watson was reassigned to special assignments under Roy Abernethy and Tom Coupe. Under American Motors' strict retirement rules, he would only be allowed to stay at AMC until June 1965, when he turned 65 years of age. He tried to interest Abernethy in letting him become a sort of roving ambassador for AMC, working the golf circuit like Buick was doing, but nothing seems to have come of that. Watson was a lifelong "saver" and when he left AMC he took many of his old Metropolitan files and photos with him. And that is how much of this book was researched, from those surviving files.

There was closure to some of the stories. The St. Louis zone eventually sold out the Met stock that had officially been *ad infinitum*. The Summer 1962 issue of the *Met Letter* was finally assembled and published by AMC enthusiast Karl Harris, although not until the summer of 1993! And all of those yellow and white Metropolitans eventually, like stray puppies, found good homes and loving families.

Tragically, James Watson and his wife died in a fire in their home in Marietta, Ohio, in January of 1990.

It has been said that one of American Motors' biggest problems was that too many of its products were ahead of their time—too advanced in concept. In November of 1995, Dale Jewett, writing about possible "cars of tomorrow" for the industry trade paper *Automotive News*, stated: "In many instances, vehicles [he meant cars of the future] will be smaller on the outside with more space on the inside for passengers. But in recognition that people spend much of their driving time traveling alone, many new vehicles will accommodate fewer passengers—typically no more than one or two."

Farewell, dear old Metropolitan. Perhaps we'll see you again in the future, where you belonged.

Chapter Six

Those Metropolitan Show Cars

Probably the most exciting Metropolitans ever built were the production-based factory show cars that first appeared in 1960 with the introduction of the fabulous Metropolitan "Fifth Avenue." The Fifth Avenue was produced especially for display at the last big auto show of the 1960 season, the colossal New York show. Painted a dazzling pearlescent pink monotone, with pink carpeting and interior trim, the Fifth Avenue was not only a radiant beauty, but also a trailblazer for the other Met show cars that would follow. Named for New York City's famed retail and theater boulevard, the Fifth Avenue set the "regional theme" that the other Met show cars would continue. It's reasonably safe to say that if the Fifth Avenue hadn't been such an enormous crowd pleaser, the rest of the specialty Mets would never have been built.

It debuted, as we said, at the last "big" show of the 1960 show season, the New York Auto Show held April 16-24, 1960, at the New York Coliseum. The *Met Letter* had this to report:

"The car is called the Fifth Avenue and in the true Easter spirit is painted Pearlescent Easter Parade Pink. The upholstery is all genuine leather—top grain cowhide in pink to match exterior of car—and the bolster area is in white pearlescent genuine leather. The car's interior is done in pink plush as is the carpeting on the turntable upon which the car revolves."

The fabulous Metropolitan Fifth Avenue. Note stuffed bunnies in car.

Metropolitan Fifth Avenue. Note hubcaps and trim rings.

The Fifth Avenue wore standard Met hubcaps enhanced by the addition of chrome "beauty" rings. To show off the rear seating area while also making the car appear roomier than it actually was, the convertible top mechanism was completely removed. It was a stunningly beautiful car.

As noted earlier, Watson and Guy Hadsall had a giveaway drawing, with stuffed pink bunnies as prizes.

The Fifth Avenue cost quite a bit to produce. When a Boston AMC dealer informed the company of his interest in purchasing the car, Watson estimated the custom work had cost AMC somewhere between $1,200-$1,400 over and above the cost of the car. That meant the cost of the customizing was roughly equal to the Met's base wholesale cost—one Met for the price of two! However, when he calculated an estimated wholesale price for the dealer, Watson proposed that AMC attempt to recover only about $398 of its customizing cost and write the rest off. As it later developed, Watson finally sold the car, presumably to the dealer he mentioned in his note, for a wholesale price of $1,845. He mentioned that the dealer felt he'd be able to retail the car for $2,495 because of its uniqueness.

Unique it was! The Fifth Avenue was a big hit at the show, creating so much interest that AMC decided to introduce other Met show cars. In fact, before the

year was out Watson had two more Met specials to show, the "Westerner" and the "Palm Beach."

Fresh and ready for the 1961 auto show circuit came the marvelous Metropolitan Westerner. It carried, obviously, the American West as its regional theme. The Westerner was painted what Watson

This view shows details of plush Fifth Avenue interior.

Wouldn't you like to get this Fifth Avenue from the Easter Bunny.

Portrait of a happy man—Met Sales Manager, Jim Watson, and the fabulous Fifth Avenue.

Fancy Met Westerner show car.

called "Palomino beige pearlescent" and was trimmed in fancy California saddle leather upholstery in brown and white with special hand tooled leather door panel inserts. Carpeting was brown and white Palomino beige plush with brown and white unborn calfskin overlays! Unlike the Fifth Avenue's standard hubcaps, the Westerner was fitted with fancy full disc wheel covers that carried the Met's trademark "M" in the center. An interesting touch was the use of metal emblems on the rear fenders. These depicted a cowgirl on a pony and were based on the famous Jordan automobile advertisement titled "Somewhere West of Laramie." Also appearing on the rear fenders was the "Westerner" name spelled out in large block letters. According to memos from Watson, the cost of producing the Westerner was rather steep—$1,073 on top of the base price of the car! But it was a dazzling automobile. Shows and Exhibits Manager Guy Hadsall recalls that at auto shows, the pretty girls who served as narrators would dress up in cowgirl outfits—provided by AMC, of course.

Also debuting as a 1961 show car was the Palm Beach, which had a Floridian theme. Painted aqua pearlescent with no contrasting color, and fitted with matching green and white genuine leather upholstery and aqua plush carpeting, the Palm Beach saw active duty on the show circuit. It later was loaned out for

appearances at selected Rambler-Metropolitan dealers. Like the Westerner, the Palm Beach wore fancy wheel covers and a metal spare tire cover. The estimated cost of producing the Palm Beach, however, was much lower. A memo from Watson to Roy Abernethy lists the cost of the custom work at a reasonable $285.65—about one-fourth of what the Westerner's custom work had cost.

The last of the "regional theme" Met show cars was also painted green, albeit a different shade from the Palm Beach. The "Cape Cod" had the Massachusetts shoreline as its theme and was painted in colors to reflect that. Its paint was called "Cape Cod pearlescent green" and the car was trimmed with matching green and white genuine leather upholstery with matching green carpeting. The *Met Letter,* Vol. 4, No. 2, noted: "A distinctive crest on the front fenders portrays the British and U.S. ensigns, symbolizing the unique Anglo-American origin of the car." Interestingly enough, some factory photos of the Cape Cod refer to it as a 1961 while others call it a 1962! The Cape Cod has a sad distinction; it was the last of the regular Met show cars that featured a regional theme.

But it wasn't the last of the special Metropolitans. There was another series of special Met show cars. Over the years, these other special Mets have been the cause of more confusion, myth and misinforma-

Metropolitan Palm Beach was another "regional theme" show car.

Another view of the Metropolitan Palm Beach.

Unique view of the Cape Cod show car—note "1961" license plate.

Cape Cod was an attractive show car.

Jim Watson, with his back to the camera, talks with AMC spokesperson Barbara Sias during an auto show that included the Met Westerner.

Advertisement for the Met Fifth Avenue.

tion than any other chapter of the Metropolitan story. These were the Royal Runabouts.

The biggest myth about the Royal Runabouts is that they were built for the British royal family and were gifted or sold to both Princess Margaret and Queen Elizabeth. Quite a glamorous myth but unfortunately, for the most part, it's false. But if we examine the core of the story we can better understand how the myths developed.

The whole impetus behind the Metropolitan Royal Runabouts came, oddly enough, from juvenile delinquency.

The Austin Division of the British Motor Corporation, the conglomerate that then encompassed most of the surviving British auto companies, presented a specially trimmed Metropolitan convertible to Prince Philip and Princess Margaret. It's believed the presentation took place sometime in 1960. The car was a mostly stock right-hand drive Austin version. It had been painted all one color, black, and was fitted with special green Vaumol Hide seat upholstery with carpets to match. This is best described as a look of "classic understated elegance" and it seems Princess Margaret especially enjoyed her little convertible.

Evidently the car appealed to young people as well, since the *London Daily Express* later reported the car was stolen by four youths! When the British press reported on the theft and subsequent stories about its recovery (only one of the errant youths was caught) they took to referring to the tiny touring car as the "royal runabout," finding humor both in the alliteration and in the idea that the royal Princess might prefer the Met over her Rolls-Royce. Princess

Side view reveals special badging and trim on the Westerner.

Three views of Princess Margaret's specially painted Metropolitan. After it was stolen, British newspapers referred to it as a "royal runabout" but it was not one of the Royal Runabout show cars.

Studio shot of the yellow Royal Runabout show car.

Margaret's car might thus be considered a runabout for royalty but it was by no means a "Royal Runabout" show car.

Soon after the theft incident, American Motors picked up the idea and took it further along the same idea track, producing two Metropolitan show cars it called the "Royal Runabouts." At first, there were only two Royal Runabouts. One was a convertible painted a medium maroon color that Watson called "Scepter Red Metallic"; 32 coats of paint were used to give it the deepest shine possible. The door notch (or reveals, as the factory often termed them) were painted Coronet Light Gold Pearlescent. The interior was fitted with leather upholstery and gold plush carpeting. Rear fenders were adorned with large script letters that spell out the words "Royal Runabout" and also carried a "crown" ornament. An extremely rare color photo of this car appears in the color section of this book.

The other Royal Runabout was a Metropolitan hardtop painted Royal Black, all one color including the roof. The door notch was Sovereign Medium Gold Pearlescent and this car, too, was equipped with leather upholstery and gold plush carpeting. In addition, it wore the "Royal Runabout" script and the crown badge on the rear fenders.

It appears that the maroon Royal Runabout was produced with no intention for it other than as a glamorous show car. The black Royal Runabout hardtop, however, was commissioned with a specific task in mind, to help the Los Angeles zone sell off some of its excessive stockpile of black and white Met hardtops. As it turned out, the Black Royal Runabout did just what it was supposed to do. Dealer and customer interest in Met hardtops shot up after the Runabout appeared, and the L.A. zone sold out its stock and

ended up having to order additional black and white hardtops to satisfy demand!

Contrary to common belief (and many published reports) there was never a black U.S. Royal Runabout convertible. A fairly common black and white photo that has appeared in several articles seems to show a black convertible with a white door notch, but this likely is a picture of the Scepter Red car—the black and white photo would make the car appear black. It's true that Princess Margaret's car was a black convertible, but her car did not have a painted door notch, was not sent to the United States, didn't have the Royal Runabout nameplate and it wasn't a true factory Royal Runabout.

There was one more Royal Runabout, perhaps the most unusual of the trio. As mentioned earlier in the book, when factory zone stock of yellow and white Metropolitans began to grow out of control, Watson commissioned another Royal Runabout for the auto show circuit. He had this last Runabout painted Gainsborough Yellow Pearlescent. Although that wasn't the same shade of yellow as the production Mets, it was hoped that dealers would paint over the white areas on stock Mets to make the cars all yellow, thus imitating the feel of the Royal Runabout if not the exact look. The yellow Royal Runabout was shown at the Chicago Auto Show, where Watson claimed it was the center of attention. It was later shown at the New York Auto Show that was held April 21-29, 1962. At the New York show the stock Mets on display were, like the yellow Runabout, hardtop models. As Watson noted, "As our soft top stocks are nil we thought it most unwise to display a convertible model."

Watson felt the "yellow job," as he termed it, was a worthy member of the Royal Runabout family and would do a good job for the company, working the

Yellow Royal Runabout as the star of a Guy Hadsall display—note small sign reads "Gainsborough Yellow Pearlescent."

Multiple views of Maurice Storck, the man who bought the yellow Royal Runabout.

auto shows and stirring up interest in Mets. So we can understand him sounding betrayed when he noted, in a May 25, 1962, report to his superiors: "You, of course, all know about the *Automotive News* story 'Production Ends For Metropolitans' which appeared in the Monday, April 23rd issue. This hit without a hint of warning to anyone in our organization and found us at the New York International Show with a special Met exhibit on the second floor and a standard Met in the other combination Rambler-Metropolitan exhibit on the third floor."

As Watson noted, the yellow Royal Runabout and the standard Met hardtop both generated considerable interest at the show. But it was too late; higher-ups had already pulled the plug on the Met.

Of this small group of special Metropolitans just discussed, something is known of the whereabouts of at least three of them. The Metropolitan Pit Stop, a restoration and parts shop in California, has the Met

Westerner. Chrysler Corporation owns the black Royal Runabout hardtop, which it acquired as an extremely small (pun intended) part of its purchase of American Motors Corporation in 1987. The Palm Beach, the Cape Cod and the maroon Royal Runabout, however, seem to have disappeared soon after their auto show service ended.

The yellow Royal Runabout has an interesting story. At one of its showings, a well-to-do businessman offered to buy the car whenever AMC wanted to dispose of it. Numbers were talked over, and a price of $3,000 was agreed upon by the businessman and an overly enthusiastic salesman who lacked the authority to bind the deal.

Trouble was, AMC wanted to send the car back to Detroit and keep it for itself. The company tried to cancel the deal. The businessman soon had his attorney file a notice of intent to sue for breach of a sales contract. AMC relented (according to the customer,

The Royal Runabouts featured plush interiors. This is the yellow car's interior.

Yellow Royal Runabout was a handsome machine.

This factory press photo is marked "1962 Cape Cod."

Factory press shot of a Royal Runabout convertible—this is most likely the maroon car. Note fancy wheel covers, painted door notch, and Royal Runabout script.

George Romney intervened and commented, "We're in business to sell cars and I'm not going to see us get sued for NOT selling a car" but we were unable to verify that account with Mr. Romney before his death in 1995). AMC finally sold the car for the agreed on $3,000 (though Watson sometimes quoted the price as $3,010). The new owner was greatly pleased with his purchase, even though it was made with full knowledge that the car was going out of production. Since that time, the yellow Royal Runabout has changed hands and is reportedly now in the northeastern United States, possibly Maine. According to some people it has since been painted black, its custom medallions are lost and its special interior has probably been destroyed. But who knows, it may turn up someday fully restored and ready to show. We were fortunate enough to find the serial number for the car—it's E90415. Someday perhaps some lucky person will come across this rare Met and return it to its original splendor. Until recently it was thought that no color photos of the car survived but we've included a few in the color section of this book.

But the biggest Met mystery of all is this one: *Whatever Happened to the Metropolitan Fifth Avenue?* The first and most famous of the Met show cars has never surfaced since it ended its show tour. A memo in the Watson files indicates that a Boston area AMC dealer was interested in it. Watson further stated that the dealer had no particular retail customer lined up for it—he simply wanted to have the car. In a note written a month later Watson mentions that he has sold the pink Met to a Boston area dealer, though he doesn't say which one. Since the car had 32 coats of lustrous pink paint, it's unlikely someone would repaint it a different color. Nor would it seem that anyone would simply junk the car—it was recognized in its time as something rare and wonderful. More likely, it was bought by someone who loved it, parked it in a cozy garage and eventually forgot about it. Perhaps that dealer bought it for himself to keep and has since lost interest in it or passed away. Hopefully he parked it in a secure storage area. It is entirely possible that this rare Met show car is resting in some dimly lit garage in Boston, patiently waiting for an enthusiast to come along who will recognize it for what it is and give it a good home. We can only hope.

Chapter Seven

Mets that Might Have Been

But what of the future? After all, every car has a future, however short its career may be. Some cars have a working-class future, such as the Chrysler K cars; some have a glamourous future, such as the Chevy Corvette; others become grand legends, such as the Ford Model A. Some cars, though, have a stillborn future, a time that doesn't come, a posterity of what-ifs and what-might-have-beens; a future clouded in mist and darkened by shadows.

For a time the world was sunny, warm and friendly and the Metropolitan's future was being plotted by some of the best minds in the business. The first Met-of-the-future appears to have been the Metro-Gnome, later renamed the Astra-Gnome, designed by Richard Arbib and displayed at the 1956 New York Auto Show. The car was so far-out that it's reasonable to guess

that it probably was never considered for production. But it's exciting regardless.

In Detroit, AMC designer Bill Reddig sketched some far-out Mets-of-the-future and luckily those drawings have survived the years. Here we can see several different directions that Met styling might have taken if only it had been allowed.

Some Met owners sent in their own styling ideas to the *Met Letter*, including one sketch shown here of a Met convertible with dual headlamps that mimic the 1957 Nash Ambassador (and the 1965-1966 Ambassador, too).

Sometimes even dealers got in on the quest for a Met-to-be. Walker Bros., a big AMC dealer in Los Angeles, sent Roy Abernethy several pictures of a Met wagon it built, reportedly with a roof made of plastic.

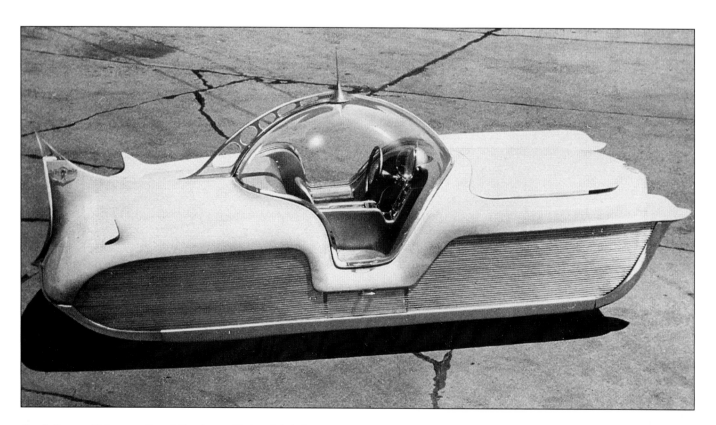

Buck Rogers' Metropolitan? Designer Richard Arbib created this "Met of the future" and displayed it at the 1956 New York Auto Show.

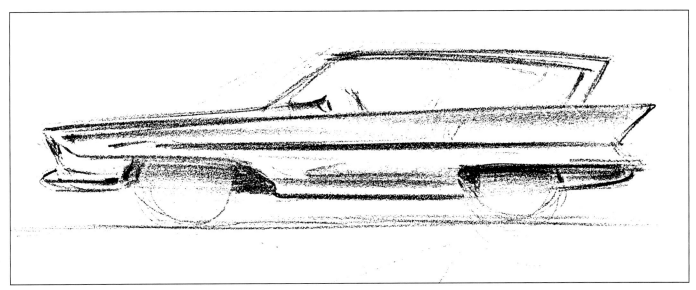

Three different sketches by AMC's Bill Reddig reveal different directions styling might have taken.

Reddig sketch shows car name shortened to "Metro."

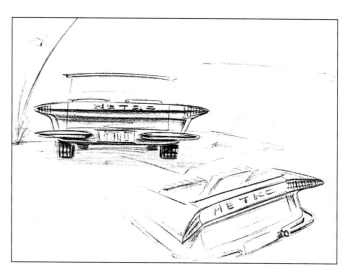

Rear view of "Metro" by Bill Reddig.

Carl Chakmakian, the AMC engineer who seems to have been everywhere and done everything connected with the Metropolitan (and a great many other AMC programs) tried to convince management to update the Met's styling a bit to keep it in line with the concurrent small Rambler. Here we see photos of two Metropolitans with their front wheel wells opened up, giving them an appearance similar to the 1955 Rambler line (later, in 1958, the small Rambler's rear wheel wells were also opened up).

Chakmakian also suggested a new top for the convertible. What he had sketched was a fabric roof that eliminated the quarter windows. The design compromised rearward visibility somewhat but was much sportier looking.

None of Chakmakian's three proposals was actually built; he simply had someone in styling cleverly retouch some factory press release photos to show what the cars could look like. It was a low cost way to present a new idea, and it's too bad AMC didn't go

Chakmakian also suggested this revised convertible top that eliminated the corner windows.

Carl Chakmakian suggested these two ideas for opening up front fenders on the Met. The convertible shows the rounded front fender opening, while the hardtop is more angular. Neither car was built. These are merely photos that were retouched.

"I liked the Met!" writes Reddig. "As you can see from the sketches, I felt the car should have a lighter, livelier, dashing look."

with the open fender look—it probably would have improved Met sales enough to keep it going a few extra years. Perhaps that extra time on the market could even have held off the Met's demise long enough for a bold new model to be introduced.

Of course, a new Met would have to sell in higher volume than the old, or it wouldn't be able to pay its tooling amortization. The cost of tooling had increased considerably in the years since the first Met was introduced. An all-new Met would have to be larger, to hold the requisite four passengers the market was now demanding. It would have the best chance of

being approved for production if it also appealed to AMC's cost accountants; possibly by being built in America, since a manufacturing profit could then be added to the ledgers. Being U.S.-built would also mean it could offer a broader range of options, including automatic transmissions, which was becoming increasingly necessary to meet changing customer demands.

In short, the Met would have to do the same thing that earlier Ramblers had done to become better sellers—it would have to become a bigger car. Such a program was certainly possible. In 1964, AMC introduced an all-new, larger Rambler American on a 106

A Met owner suggested this idea with front fenders and quad headlamps that mimic the 1958 Ambassador as well as the 1965/66 Ambassador.

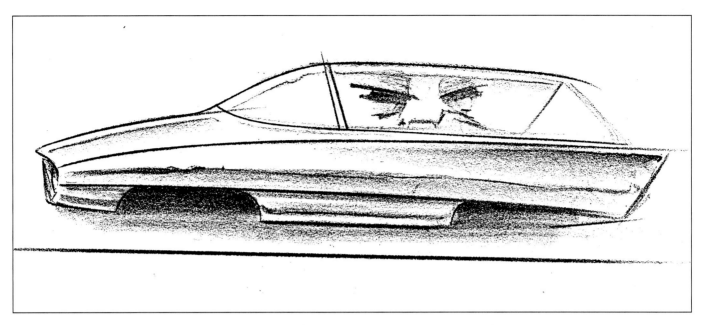

Another Reddig idea was a rear-facing seat. Note "C" pillar shows similarity to later Gremlin.

inch wheelbase. At the same time the old 100 inch wheelbase chassis ended production. If AMC wanted to introduce a new Met, it could have restyled the 1961-1963 American 100 inch chassis one more time, coming up with what then would be the lowest priced car in its lineup: a 1964 Rambler Metropolitan, made in America.

The old American convertible body could have been fitted with a manual top, rather than its electric top, to reduce costs. The flathead six and three-speed transmission would have been an ideal low-cost drivetrain. The 1963 American hardtop body could have been restyled to make a new Met hardtop. And obviously, in later years a Met wagon based on the American two-door wagon could have been introduced.

The new Met could have become a member of the Rambler family of cars, much as the 1958-1961 "Ambassador by Rambler" became simply the Rambler Ambassador in 1962. The new AMC lineup could have consisted of the Rambler Metropolitan on the restyled 100 inch wheelbase, the all-new Teague-designed Rambler American on the 106 inch wheelbase, plus the Rambler Classics and Ambassadors on the 112 inch wheelbase.

Such an expansion of the Rambler line would have been a positive move, rather than the approach Abernethy later took when he began to restrict the Rambler brand to only lower priced cars.

It might have worked. Who can say for certain?

Edmund Anderson, the last head of Nash Styling and first head of AMC styling, was a Nash-Healey enthusiast (like Chakmakian). But Anderson evidently must have had some thought about styling a new Metropolitan for the 1960s. A workflow chart for the styling studios, which Anderson sent to us shortly before his death, indicates a possible new Metropolitan, dubbed the "Y" program, for 1962/63. An obscure

1962 memo to Roy Abernethy makes mention of a study of the market for a car priced under $1,700 and it, too, refers to a "Y" car. Unfortunately, neither of these provides any details whatsoever as to what the new car would have looked like. Thus far, no other information has surfaced.

But these "programs" were only pen and pencil ideas. Nothing significant was built from those ideas and nothing further ever became of them. There was, however, a real, honest-to-goodness Met of the future. The factory even had two of them built for evaluation. These were the wonderful Metropolitan station wagons.

The Met wagons were conceived by AM Styling as a low cost solution to the Metropolitan's twin problems of seating capacity and trunk space. The concept fit right in with the direction AMC was taking in the mid-fifties; a large percentage of its mainline Rambler models were station wagon-type vehicles. In fact, AMC was enjoying an unusually large share of the station wagon market. It seemed to make sense to extend the wagon concept down to the lowest priced cars in its lineup. To keep tooling costs to a minimum, the Met wagons would be built on a modified Met chassis.

One drawback to offering a low priced Met wagon was that it might steal away sales from the larger, more profitable Rambler American wagon, or even from the bigger Ramblers. And there is no doubt that the Met wagon would have been low-priced; Watson expected it to retail for the same price tag as the Met hardtop! At that price, it would most likely cannibalize sales of the hardtop, since it would offer four-passenger seating and a larger cargo carrying capability for the same money.

The Met wagons are often referred to as 1960 models but that's not really accurate. There were two built; the more commonly known of the pair wore a

This proposal for a Met wagon was built by AMC. Note early style grille, Nash hubcaps and grille badge. Note also the interesting hood ornament and side moldings.

Rear view of wagon proposal. Note how the roof line is similar to 1961/63 Rambler American. This proposal lacks a tailgate, but has an opening rear window.

Nash emblem in its grille and carried the zigzag side trim. Its serial number indicates it was built in mid-1956. The other of the pair wore a 1954/55 style grille, so it wouldn't be a 1960 model either. Neither car had vent windows, so obviously they both were pre-1959 cars. However, the wagon design may have been planned as a 1960 model, so only in that sense would the 1960 designation be appropriate.

We talked with the man who designed them, AMC's Bill Reddig. Reddig was hired as a designer by Nash and stayed with the company when it became AMC. He worked on the landmark 1956 Rambler and other successful Rambler designs and also the Metropolitan. Although Reddig transferred over to Kelvinator at the tail end of 1958, before leaving he had worked on the design of the Met wagons. Upon acceptance of the final design, AMC had Pininfarina build a prototype. Reddig later explained that Pininfarina was chosen because that firm could deliver a handmade prototype faster and at much lower cost than American firms could. Besides, AMC already had a relationship with the famed Italian designer. The other wagon is believed to have been built by AMC.

Guy Hadsall was in on some of the discussions about the wagons and recalled this: "I ... can tell you some info on the proposed Met wagon. We had a number of meetings where it was discussed and voted upon as to whether we would favor the Met wagon or bring back the 100 inch Rambler. We did not have budget enough to do both. The difference was that the Rambler 100 inch would be built in Kenosha, and be available in several body styles. The Met would be an import and one body style. We all wanted both as they were really two different markets. But if we could have only one then the Rambler 100 was the most logical choice."

Of the two prototype wagons that were built only the Pininfarina car survives today. At the time of this writing it was in the collection of Jim Valentine, owner of a Metropolitan parts and repair business in California. The other car, according to Ed Anderson, was sold to AMC designer Dick Teague. Supposedly, the car was later destroyed in an accident.

There were even some rumors of a Met powered by an air-cooled engine. That actually had some basis in reality, more than one would suspect at first. The Volkswagen Beetle was the top selling import in America and tended to dominate the thinking of its competitors. Proof of that can be seen in Chevrolet's introduction of the rear-engined, air-cooled Corvair to counter the VW's sales inroads. AMC ordinarily wouldn't have considered a small car program that required a special engine, since the tooling costs would have swamped it. But as it turned out, AMC already had an air-cooled small car engine right on the shelf. The engine had been designed for the Mighty Mite

Often referred to as a 1960 model, this Metropolitan station wagon prototype was built by Pininfarina on a 1956 chassis. Note Nash grille badge, lack of vent windows.

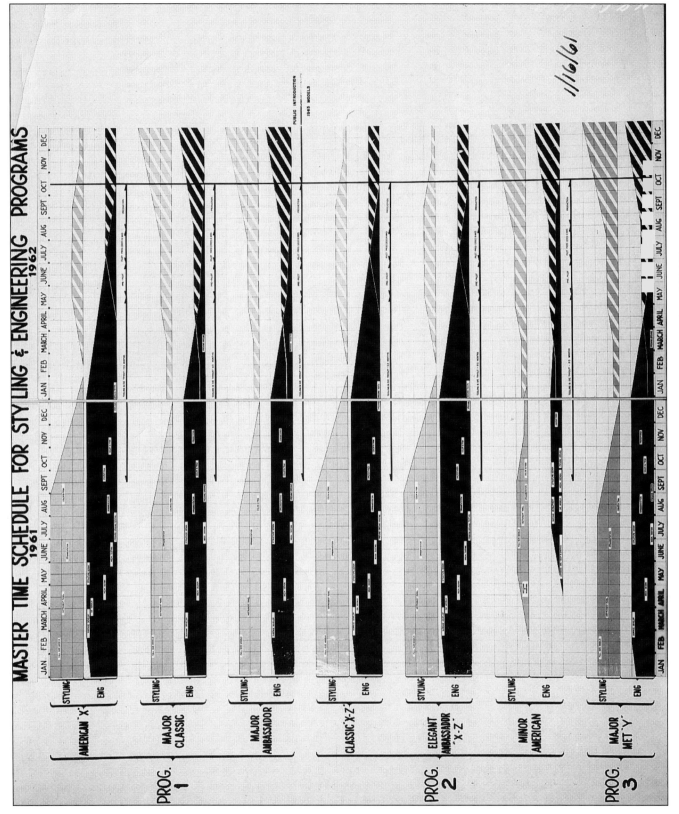

Never before published view of AMC styling schedule shows new Met was planned for 1961/62.

This concept, drawn in 1996 by retired AMC designer Bill Reddig, shows one possible way the Metropolitan could have been updated for 1963/64. Reddig retained the original chassis dimensions, but restyled the fenders to bring the appearance closer to that of the 1960 Rambler American. The roof is completely redone, greatly increasing interior space so that four passengers could ride with reasonable comfort.

small four-wheel-drive vehicle that AMC developed for the military. The Mighty Mite's engine was an aluminum alloy air-cooled V-4 that generated 62 horsepower and offered light weight and terrific durability.

Jim Watson even hinted at the possibility in a letter he wrote to a Met owner in Tennessee. "It is interesting," he wrote, "to note that you were considering buying a Volkswagen prior to your purchase of a Metropolitan ... your suggestion that an air-cooled engine would be desirable in the Metropolitan is most interesting. As you may know, we are now in the process of getting ready to build 250 Mighty Mite lightweight vehicles for the U.S. Marine Corps. These jobs weigh about 1,500 pounds and will be powered by a V-4 cylinder direct air-cooled aluminum engine that has been designed by our engineers. This engine will develop approximately 62 horsepower and it would appear that it might have some interesting possibilities for the future."

Even George Romney was reported to have said the Mighty Mite's engine could possibly show up in a small passenger car. According to one magazine, AMC did build a Metropolitan test car with the air-cooled V-4. However, AMC engineer Carl Chakmakian doesn't recall ever seeing such a machine. At this time it's not certain if the idea was given serious consideration. Perhaps more information will surface someday.

It's interesting to note that of the ideas that appeared for a new Met, most were for four-passenger designs. The only one that was built, shown to the public and discussed seriously by AMC planners was the four-passenger wagon. It would seem, then, that even if the Met had survived, it most likely would have become a bit more practical. We asked Bill Reddig to sketch an idea of what the next generation of Metropolitan might have looked like if it retained its original wheelbase, and it is shown here for the first time.

Chapter Eight

Tips for the Metropolitan Enthusiast

By Karl Harris

Collecting and restoring your Metropolitan will be a most rewarding experience. No matter where you drive or show your Met, it will turn heads and stimulate much interest. No matter what car the Metropolitan is up against, there is always that magical soft spot that draws any old car enthusiast to it. To this day Metropolitan owners write and talk about their little jewels just as the original owners did over 35 years ago.

The popularity of the Metropolitan has steadily increased, particularly in recent years. No wonder! No

The owner of this Met modified its steering wheel.

Photos from Met owners who wrote in to AMC.

other car has the class, elegance or uniqueness of the Metropolitan. Collectors love its small size, which minimizes storage concerns. Its economy and high gas mileage fit well in today's environmental philosophy.

Virtually all mechanical parts are available for the restoration of your Metropolitan. This is because the British manufacturers used many of the same Metropolitan parts in their other production cars. Some of the parts are still being used in today's vehicles. Interest in British collector cars such as the Triumph, Spitfire or MG, which used many of the same parts used in the Metropolitan, has created a sufficient demand for the reproduction of those parts no longer in regular use. The body parts are the only more challenging parts to find.

Attending car shows to scour for parts and literature always proves fun and exciting, particularly when that elusive part or that rare piece of literature is found. However, car shows are only a small part of the restoration process. Publications, technical guides, parts sources, owner fellowship and literature of the period are all part of the equation for the successful restoration of your Metropolitan.

Much information exists on all general aspects of collector car restoration. Books such as *Standard Guide to Automotive Restoration* or *Wired for Success* (Krause Publications, 800-258-0929) are excellent general references for learning all of the basic requirements for restoring your Metropolitan. Joining a multi-make car club is also useful for general restoration guidance and fellowship. This chapter will attempt to help the new Metropolitan enthusiast with some basic tips and to point out those little peculiarities specific to the Met.

The first tip any experienced automobile enthusiast will suggest is to:

Join a Club that Specializes in the Marque

This is by far the most valuable tip that can be given to the new old car enthusiast, and of course holds true for any make automobile. For the Metropolitan, there are several clubs to consider joining in addition to the one bearing its marque. This is because Metropolitan production spanned the years just before and just after the merger of Nash and Hudson, which of course formed AMC.

Photos (this page) from Met owners who wrote in to AMC.

The marque clubs for the Metropolitan are the Metropolitan Owners' Club of North America (United States) and the Metropolitan Owners' Club (United Kingdom). The seeds of these clubs were first sown in August of 1972 when the Metropolitan Owners' Club (MOC) was formed in England by W. E. "Bill" Dowsing. MOC is recognized as the first club devoted to preserving the Metropolitan marque. At the time this British club was formed, the average sale price for a good Metropolitan in Great Britain was $155 and rough versions could be had for $17! Jim Watson was made an honorary member of the MOC club (member #108). To join the club write to: MOC Secretary, South Cottage, School Lane, Washington, Pulborough, West Sussex, RH20 4AP, England.

C. R. "Dick" Maize of Somerset, Pennsylvania, was an integral member of this British club (member #126), but he soon saw the need for such a club in the

United States. With much initiative, Maize founded the Metropolitan Owners' Club of North America, or MOCNA, which was and still is distinct from the British MOC.

In MOCNA's first newsletter dated February 1, 1975, Maize wrote, "Already we have 22 dues-paying members, and 15 or so applications in the mail to people who have seen our ad in various antique automobile magazines." He followed with "Several members have written telling how they gained fame and recognition because they are owners of Metropolitans." This new newsletter had thus picked up the regular publication of the many interesting testimonials enthusiastically provided by Metropolitan owners that had been the role of the *Met Letter* some thirteen years before. This newsletter evolved into the monthly publication known today as *The Met Gazette*. This award-winning black and white publication has become the trademark of MOCNA.

One can imagine Jim Watson's personal pleasure when he received his first newsletter of the newly formed MOCNA mailed to him on February 3, 1975. This was ten years after his retirement from AMC and thirteen years after the demise of the Metropolitan and the *Met Letter* publication. Yes, Jim still had his Met. It was listed in the 1976 and 1977 MOC Rosters as model # "SPL" registration #B-370646 (Michigan), 1956 model year and yellow in color. Presumably, the Model # "SPL" referred to a "special" model; in this

case, Watson's car had twin carburetors. Today, it is believed that his special Met resides in the collection of the Metropolitan Pit Stop, which is a specialty parts and restoration business located in California.

Today, MOCNA has a membership of approximately 2,400 from all over the world and has many chapters spanning the United States and Canada. The club not only provides the monthly *Met Gazette* but also valuable information including restoration guidance, parts sources and advertisements all specific to the Metropolitan. To join the club write to the MOCNA Membership Chairman, 5009 Barton Road, Madison, WI 53711. Dues are $15/year.

Another club to consider joining is the Nash Car Club of America. This club publishes bimonthly *The Nash Times* and an advertising bulletin in the other months. This club specializes in Nash production automobiles and the Metropolitan. The club often publishes Metropolitan information and restoration tips as well as parts sources and owner advertising. To join the club write to P.O. Box 80279, Dept. H, Indianapolis, IN 46280. Dues are $23/year.

A third club to consider joining is the AMC Rambler Club. This club publishes the *Rambler Reader* quarterly and an advertising bulletin monthly. The club specializes in all AMC production between the years 1958 and 1969, which are the years of the AMC Rambler. The club recognizes all Metropolitans and often publishes Metropolitan information along with parts sources and restoration tips. To join the club write to 2645 Ashton Road, Cleveland Heights, OH 44118. Basic dues are $18/year.

A fourth club to consider is the Hudson-Essex-Terraplane Club. This club specializes in Hudson and Essex and Terraplane production automobiles and recognizes all Metropolitans. It publishes the *White Triangle News*, which often includes Metropolitan information, parts sources and owner advertising. To join the club write to 100 East Cross Street, Ypsilanti, MI 48198. Dues are $20/year.

Other clubs that recognize the Metropolitan include AMC World Clubs, which is devoted to those enthusiasts interested in all of the AMC cars produced from 1955 to 1988 (write to 7963 Depew Street, Arvada, CO 80003) and American Motors Owners Association, which is devoted to all of the AMC cars produced from 1955 to 1988 (write to 6756 Cornell Street, Portage, MI 49002).

These and other clubs not listed here typically advertise in national antique automobile publications, which leads to another tip:

Subscribe to a Collector Car Publication

A number of fine publications are dedicated to the general antique automobile enthusiast. Publications, such as *Old Cars Weekly News & Marketplace, Hemmings Motor News, Skinned Knuckles* or *Cars & Parts* offer much information, parts and literature sources, restoration tips and reproduction sources that are of general usefulness to the Met enthusiast. Often, Metropolitan cars, parts or literature will be advertised by their owners only in these general publications as they are not aware of the existence of the clubs. Most old car collectors find that receiving one or more general publications coupled with a club membership is most beneficial for their restoration and collecting efforts.

Having joined a club and upon receipt of your materials, the next step is to find that Metropolitan with your name on it, which leads to the next tip:

Evaluate Your New Metropolitan Carefully

There are many stories throughout the collector car hobby of purchasing that special collector car, only to find hidden problems that are costly to repair. "Buyer beware" continues to be the age-old advice in this regard, and the Metropolitan is no exception.

The value of your Metropolitan depends critically on its condition. To aid you in determining its value, publications, such as the bimonthly *Old Cars Price Guide*, list up-to-date valuations typically based on auction results, known private sales, and expert opinions. Of course the true value of a car is the price the buyer and seller agree upon; the published guides should only be used to focus on a "ballpark" value.

As with any other old car, the Metropolitan has its share of common rust problem areas that should always be checked and thoroughly evaluated before making a purchase offer. Fortunately, all of the problem rust areas are relatively easy to spot from underneath, and there is often tell-tale evidence of deterioration associated with these problem areas.

The first problem rust areas to check are the door posts. Water, mud, salt and other debris can splash into the supports wreaking havoc on these metal supports, particularly on the driver's side. If you can see sun or the pavement while looking through the holes where the door hinges go through, inspect the area carefully from underneath and check for door sag. Such a condition would suggest the likelihood that some expensive welding reinforcement will be required to repair the situation.

The second problem rust area to check is the dash and toeboard assembly, i.e. firewall. In particular, check the area behind the wiring harness, which may require the removal of the harness for an unobstructed view of the firewall. When new, the Metropolitan had a plastic hose that would direct water away from the windshield area and the engine compartment and down to the roadway below. This tube typically deteriorated, allowing the water to collect in the region behind the wiring harness along the firewall. If unchecked, this can lead to potentially serious firewall deterioration that can be tricky and somewhat expensive to fix as the firewall is an integral part of the unitbody construction.

The third problem rust area to check is the floor pan. The Met's step-down design coupled with no

Body Identification

Identifying the original body style and paint scheme of your Metropolitan can be accomplished by interpreting the codes on the chassis number plate and the body number plate, both of which are located on the right side of the dash under the hood. These are described in the Metropolitan Technical Service Manual from which sections are reproduced below.

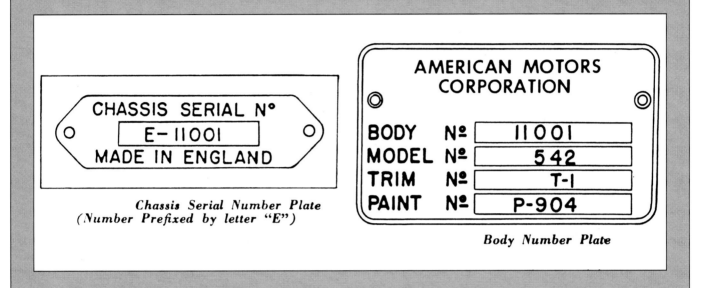

Chassis Serial Number Plate
(Number Prefixed by letter "E")

Body Number Plate

The model year is not indicated on these identification plates because this was solely determined by the date of sale as has already been described in previous chapters.

According to the technical service manual, two body styles were available: the hardtop and the convertible soft top. Listed below are the Model and Series identifications.

Model	Series	Starting Serial Number
541 Convertible	A	(E-1001
542 Hardtop	A	("
541 Convertible	B	(E-11001
542 Hardtop	B	("
561 Convertible	1500	(E-21008
562 Hardtop	1500	("

The body number plate lists the body, model, trim and paint identification numbers. All of the color names and sources are available today through MOCNA.

The paint code number as shown on the body number plate and the color name of the paint were required to obtain paint from the manufacturer for repairs. This is because some of the cars were painted two-tone and unless the color name was given, it would not be known which color was desired. The manual gave an example of this: "For example: Paint No. P904. This would indicate the complete car was painted in one color (Canyon Red). Paint No. P903-7. This would indicate the lower color was No. P903 (Spruce Green) and the upper color No. P907 (Mist Gray)."

drain holes led to easy accumulation of water under the rubber mats and carpet from normal use and from leaks. Such dampness can lead to serious deterioration of the floor pan. Be sure to inspect the floor pan thoroughly from the top and underneath. It is expensive to replace a deteriorated floor pan, particularly since it is an integral part of the unit-body construction.

The last problem rust areas are the channel reinforcements and the side sill assemblies. These are the two double-walled frame supports below each of the doors on the underside of the body. Here too, the driver's side tends to be worse than the passenger side. These support the weight of the car; if rusted badly, they will cause the car to sag in the middle and the doors will not open and close freely. This is more critical for convertibles since the hardtop roof helps to support the car.

And speaking of convertibles, it is wise to verify that your convertible Met is not a modified hardtop. A good way to check for this is to look for the small spring-loaded wedge-type latch located about one-quarter of the way down along the edge of door above the door lock. The mating wedge-type latch is located in the matching position on the door pillar. This wedge-type latch system, which was designed to help keep the convertible doors from opening unexpectedly, was an added safety feature found only on the convertible. The absence of this extra latch system on a "convertible" would suggest that that car was originally a hardtop.

If the typical problem rust areas show little or no signs of deterioration, then your potential new Metropolitan is likely to be a solid car. The next step is to evaluate the rest of the body, mechanics and driveability using your own experience, or that of a fellow enthusiast or mechanic.

Once you have acquired your Metropolitan, the next step is to address the mechanical problems so that your car is up and running to get you to that next car show! A helpful aid at this point would be to:

Obtain a Copy of the Metropolitan Technical Service Manual

The technical service manual is an extensive book used by mechanics that describes in detail most of the repair procedures, assembly/disassembly procedures, specifications and maintenance procedures. The Metropolitan was no exception. The first Metropolitan technical service manual was the Nash Technical Service Manual for the NKI Models 541-542 (Nash publication number NAS 53-1480-10M-1053) published late in 1953. When the name Metropolitan was created on January 22, 1954, dealers and service garages would simply write or stamp the word "Metropolitan" on these first issue manuals.

Since the Metropolitan did not change much with each model year, only a few versions of the technical service manual were produced. Interestingly, in 1979

AMC published a technical service manual covering all six models of the Metropolitan (AMC publication #AM-79-7043). This publication was essentially a reprint of the earlier publications that combined the common technical details of all the models with those specific to each model. Since the original technical service manuals had become rather scarce, it is possible that Metropolitan enthusiasts, particularly those who had become members of the fledging MOCNA, contributed to the demand that led AMC to produce this 1979 reprint of the Metropolitan Technical Service Manual.

It is helpful to remember that although the Metropolitan was an AMC design, it is a British built car. This means that restoration of the Metropolitan is similar to that of other British built cars. A good example of this is the Metropolitan's electrical system, which is a positive ground system using three wires. The third wire is the grounding wire typical of British-made cars. The electrical system will work properly only if there is a solid connection made to ground.

Specific mechanics to address for the Metropolitan are not unlike that of any other collector car. The goal is to be able to start and stop your car reliably and keep it running in between. This means the major mechanical systems to address include the electrical, brake, cooling and fuel systems. All components of these systems should be inspected and replaced, with the focus on *replace* if the parts are old. All the lines should be flushed and/or blown out. All fluids and filters should be replaced with new fluids and filters.

Regular maintenance is also required to keep your restoration running smoothly. To help with this, a Lubrication Service Chart and Capacities table was printed in the technical service manuals and the owner's manuals. A reproduction of the ones found in the 1979 technical service manual reprint is pictured. Such servicing was recommended to be performed every 1,000 miles for most items.

Mechanical restoration work clearly relies heavily on a good source of parts and services offered, which leads to our next tip:

Find Good Parts and Service Sources

Here is where membership to a club that recognizes the marque can be invaluable. All of those small collector hoards and all the major dealers can typically be found in club literature. The fellowship with other Met owners will invariably lead to that one elusive part needed to put the final touches on your restoration or that key troubleshooting tip. Personal testimonials from other Met owners will also lead to those trustworthy services, ranging from the rebuilding of key mechanical components to cosmetic restoration work. Whether you are a restoration novice or expert, a good source of parts and services offered is essential to the successful restoration of your Metropolitan.

Metropolitan Lubrication Service Chart

LUBRICATE AT EACH ARROW POINT EVERY 1,000 MILES EXCEPT AS NOTED

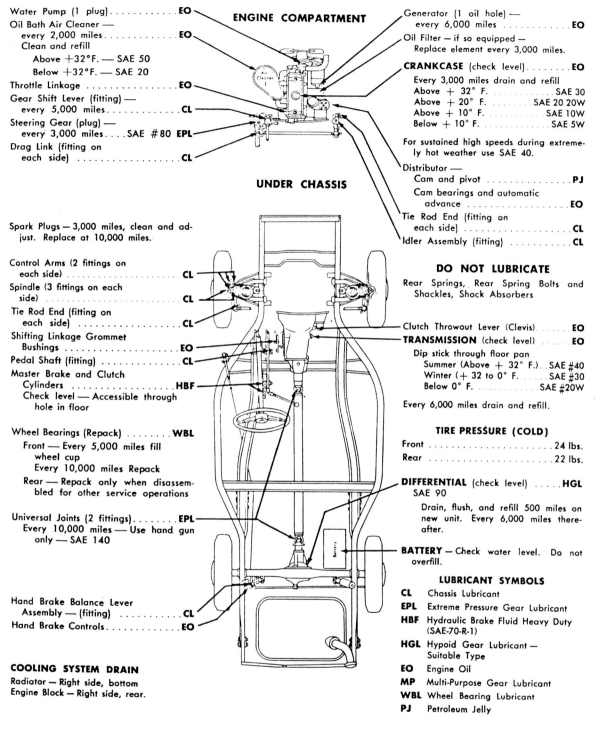

ENGINE COMPARTMENT

Water Pump (1 plug)............**EO**
Oil Bath Air Cleaner —
  every 2,000 miles............**EO**
  Clean and refill
    Above +32°F. — SAE 50
    Below +32°F. — SAE 20
Throttle Linkage ....**EO**
Gear Shift Lever (fitting) —
  every 5,000 miles.............**CL**
Steering Gear (plug) —
  every 3,000 miles....SAE #80 **EPL**
Drag Link (fitting on
  each side) ....**CL**

UNDER CHASSIS

Spark Plugs — 3,000 miles, clean and ad-
  just. Replace at 10,000 miles.

Control Arms (2 fittings on
  each side) ....**CL**
Spindle (3 fittings on each
  side) ....**CL**
Tie Rod End (fitting on
  each side) ....**CL**
Shifting Linkage Grommet
  Bushings ....**EO**
Pedal Shaft (fitting) ....**CL**
Master Brake and Clutch
  Cylinders ....**HBF**
  Check level — Accessible through
  hole in floor

Wheel Bearings (Repack) ....**WBL**
  Front — Every 5,000 miles fill
  wheel cup
  Every 10,000 miles Repack
  Rear — Repack only when disassem-
  bled for other service operations

Universal Joints (2 fittings)......**EPL**
  Every 10,000 miles — Use hand gun
  only — SAE 140

Hand Brake Balance Lever
  Assembly — (fitting) ....**CL**
Hand Brake Controls............**EO**

COOLING SYSTEM DRAIN
Radiator — Right side, bottom
Engine Block — Right side, rear.

Generator (1 oil hole) —
  every 6,000 miles ....**EO**
Oil Filter — if so equipped —
  Replace element every 3,000 miles.
CRANKCASE (check level).......**EO**
  Every 3,000 miles drain and refill
  Above + 32° F. ....SAE 30
  Above + 20° F. ......SAE 20 20W
  Above + 10° F. ....SAE 10W
  Below + 10° F. ....SAE 5W

For sustained high speeds during extremely hot weather use SAE 40.

Distributor —
  Cam and pivot ....**PJ**
  Cam bearings and automatic
    advance ....**EO**
Tie Rod End (fitting on
  each side) ....**CL**
Idler Assembly (fitting) ....**CL**

DO NOT LUBRICATE

Rear Springs, Rear Spring Bolts and
Shackles, Shock Absorbers

Clutch Throwout Lever (Clevis) .....**EO**
TRANSMISSION (check level) .....**EO**
  Dip stick through floor pan
  Summer (Above + 32° F.) .SAE #40
  Winter (+ 32 to 0° F. .....SAE #30
  Below 0° F. ....SAE #20W

Every 6,000 miles drain and refill.

TIRE PRESSURE (COLD)
Front ....24 lbs.
Rear ....22 lbs.

DIFFERENTIAL (check level) .....**HGL**
SAE 90
  Drain, flush, and refill 500 miles on
  new unit. Every 6,000 miles there-
  after.

BATTERY — Check water level. Do not
overfill.

LUBRICANT SYMBOLS
CL   Chassis Lubricant
EPL Extreme Pressure Gear Lubricant
HBF Hydraulic Brake Fluid Heavy Duty
       (SAE-70-R-1)
HGL Hypoid Gear Lubricant —
       Suitable Type
EO   Engine Oil
MP   Multi-Purpose Gear Lubricant
WBL Wheel Bearing Lubricant
PJ   Petroleum Jelly

CAPACITIES

MEASURE SYSTEM	CRANKCASE Quarts		TRANSMISSION Pints	DIFFERENTIAL Pints	COOLING SYSTEM		GAS TANK Gallons
	Less Filter	With Filter			With Heater Quarts	Without Heater Quarts	
U.S.A.	4	4½	5½	2¼	8	7	10½
British Imperial	3⅓	3¾	4½	1¾	6⅔	5⅞	8¾

When your Metropolitan has been put into dependable driving condition, the last step is to complete the cosmetics of the car. As pointed out earlier, many publications exist discussing general sheet metal repairs, painting and other related restoration topics and will not be discussed here. But, in order to complete the small details specific to the Metropolitan you will need to acquire:

Access to Promotional and Dealer Literature

Metropolitan literature, such as dealer advertisements, flyers, advertising folders, press releases, mechanical bulletins, technical service manuals, owner's manuals, posters and magazine reviews are highly collectible and are enjoyable even without owning a Metropolitan. Owning or having access to this literature is a big help in restoring your Metropolitan to the condition it was in at the time it was first sold. Original literature, such as factory photos, specifications, available accessories, and paint schemes, illustrate the critical details required to restore your Metropolitan to its original appearance.

Again, this is where a club or national publications can help out. Antique automobile literature dealers continuously trade in Metropolitan literature. Those hard-to-find literature items can often be obtained as reproductions or as a handbook compiled by volunteer members of the clubs. Scouring dealer stocks at car shows for these elusive items can often be rewarding as well, as Metropolitan literature is generally scarcer than the more common marques.

And when you show your Metropolitan, you can also display the literature you have acquired. This will complete your display and will be helpful when you talk about your car and its history to that novice Metropolitan enthusiast, like you once were.

Today's Metropolitan enthusiasts enjoy their cars much as the original owners did some 35-40 years ago. Met testimonials are still being written and published in the *Met Gazette* as they were long ago in the *Met Letter*. Virtually all parts, with the exception of body parts, are available, which eases the restoration process. No other car offers its owner the charm, uniqueness, attention from others and ability to relive the past as the Metropolitan.

Chapter Nine

Sales and Production

In writing automotive history, one has to be careful about how numbers are presented. As a longtime AMC writer, I can attest to the difficulty of sorting out conflicting numbers for sales, production, and registrations. Sales figures would seem to be straightforward enough, since they represent sales of cars. But what tends to complicate any study of AMC sales numbers is that sometimes the figures represent retail sales to the public and other times they represent wholesale sales to dealers (the latter are most often shown in the company's annual report). Further complicating any comparison of year-to-year results is that sometimes they're listed by calendar year, sometimes by model year (all 1960 models, for example) and often by the company's fiscal year. To further confuse the subject, AMC's fiscal year ran from October to September for the years 1954 through 1979, after which it was changed to a straight calendar year basis.

In the case of the Metropolitan, comparison is made even more complex because AMC also listed Met shipments. Shipments were the actual transfer of the car from England to the country it would be sold in.

Confused? Consider this: it took the authors nearly six months of research to compile a summary of Metropolitan retail sales by calendar year. The numbers shown here are the most accurate we've seen and can be considered reliable.

Domestic Retail Sales of Metropolitans by Calendar Year
Includes U.S. sales only

1954	7,579	includes Hudson Metropolitans
1955	6,262	includes Hudson Metropolitans
1956	7,323	
1957	12,226	
1958	12,681	
1959	14,959	
1960	11,689	
1961	8,881	
1962	2,428	

Total U.S. retail sales: 84,028

According to the *Met Gazette*, of the 10,000 A series Mets built, 6,083 were hardtops and 3,917 were convertibles. Of the 94,968 total Mets produced for North America, 75,569 were hardtops and 19,399 were convertibles.

The numbers most Met enthusiasts are familiar with are the aforementioned shipments, and we've included them here since they also show the number of Mets shipped to Canada. At this time we don't know how many Mets were retailed in Canada, but we assume it must have been close to the number shipped there. Any discrepancy would probably be units that were re-shipped for sale in other Commonwealth countries, or perhaps even to the U.S.

Met owners and their cars.

Metropolitan Shipments from Inception

Calendar Year	U.S. Year	U.S. — Cum.	Canada & Export Year	Canada & Export — Cum.	Total Year	Total — Cum.
1953	571	571	172	172	743	743
1954	11,198	11,769	1,964	2,136	13,162	13,905
1955	3,849	15,618	2,247	4,383	6,096	20,001
1956	7,645	23,263	1,423	5,806	9,068	29,069
1957	13,425	36,688	1,892	7,698	15,317	44,386
1958	11,951	48,639	1,177	8,875	13,128	57,514
1959	20,435	69,074	1,774	10,649	22,209	79,723
1960	13,103	82,177	771	11,420	13,874	93,597
1961	853	83,030	116	11,536	969	94,566
1962	412	83,442	8	11,544	420	94,986

These numbers were copied from a famous AMC memo and are believed accurate. The numbers do not include sales of Austin Metropolitans. Opinions vary as to how many Metropolitans were sold by Austin. It is unlikely the exact number will ever be determined, since the Austin Mets did not have serial numbers that ran in sequence, as did the U.S. cars. Metropolitans produced for sale through Austin dealers were assigned Austin serial numbers on an apparently random basis. One noted British historian gave an estimate of perhaps 9,400 Austin Metropolitans, adding that Austin sold the car throughout the United Kingdom and also other European countries as well as South Africa. It appears certain that Rambler dealers in some European countries sold U.S.-type Metropolitans, sometimes in competition with Austin dealers who were selling Austin Metropolitans (apparently the Austins were available with either right- or left-hand steering, depending on which market the car was sold in).

As we noted in the main text, model years for Mets were determined by the date of the sale of the car new at retail. Jim Watson offered this guide:

All Metropolitans sold new at retail on or after

Nov. 26, 1954, were registered as 1955 models.
Dec. 15, 1955, were registered as 1956 models.
Oct. 25, 1956, were registered as 1957 models.
Oct. 22, 1957, were registered as 1958 models.
Oct. 8, 1958, were registered as 1959 models.
Oct. 14, 1959, were registered as 1960 models.
Oct. 12, 1960, were registered as 1961 models.
Oct. 6, 1961, were registered as 1962 models.

Apparently, someone wrote in to Watson asking if his Met could be considered a 1963 model. Watson explained the company's long standing policy of registering existing stock as current model year effective on the date of new car announcement and wrote: "In other words if you purchased your Metropolitan as a brand new car in January 1963 it would still be designated as a 1962 model. The highest Metropolitan serial number was 95,986. Engine #34760." The reasoning was that because there was never a 1963 announcement, there was no 1963 Met, regardless if any were sold in 1963.

It has been written in several magazine articles, including one by the author of this book, Patrick R. Foster, that Met production ceased in the spring of 1960. We now believe that information was incorrect. Recently discovered factory memos indicate Metropolitan production continued to 1961, ending finally on April 15, 1961. Dealer and zone stocks, plus a healthy number of Mets in storage in England, provided enough inventory for sales to continue through 1962.

Chapter Ten

Epilogue

So ends the Metropolitan story, or at least its early history. But the legend will continue, because an admiring public will simply not allow these delightful cars to be forgotten. The Met will live forever, a gentle memory of a very happy time. The role it plays now is to prod us occasionally from our complacency, like an excited puppy that delights in walking with its master. "Come" says the little Met, "let's go for a spin."

Over the many months it took to write this book, with nineteen hour work days stretching before me like sand dunes, I was often cheered by reading the wonderful letters sent in to AMC from enthusiastic Met owners. These letters, brittle now with age, brought many smiles to my face and much warmth to my heart. We'll end the book with quotes from a representative letter, written by the lovely lady pictured here.

Farewell!

Dear Sir,

...I feel that I just have to write and tell you how thrilled I am with this little Nash car. It is so much more fun to drive, and it is such a comfortable car to ride in. I can at last park in a small place which I could never do with a large car. It is simply a beautiful car in style, color and performance. I ... think it outranks all large cars. Since 1918 I have driven a Ford, Chevrolet, Franklin, Chandler, Plymouth, Pontiac and a Packard and now this beautiful little Nash which I prize above them all....

Sincerely,
Mrs. Ben Moore

Thanks Met lovers and may God bless you all!

Patrick R. Foster
August 1996

About the Authors

Author Pat Foster, right, chats with former Nash/AMC designer Bill Reddig at the Easter Region Nash Meet in Burlington, Vermont, 1995. (Photo courtesy W. Scott Cameron.)

Patrick Foster's byline is well known to most American Motors enthusiasts. He has been writing about AMC for several years and his articles have appeared in numerous magazines including *Automobile Quarterly, AutoWeek, Collectible Automobile* and *Special Interest Autos*. A longtime AMC collector, Patrick currently owns three Ramblers of various vintage. His first book, *American Motors The Last Independent*, won acclaim for its in-depth examination of the company's history. Pat is a member of the board of directors of the Society of Automotive Historians.

Born in Burlington, Vermont, Patrick has spent most of his life in the seaside town of Milford, Connecticut, "one of the greatest little towns in the country," he claims. He resides there with his wife Diane, daughter Caitlin and Samantha the cat. Among the many projects he plans to work on in the future are a book on Jeep and one covering American Motors dream cars, limited-issue and concept cars.

Karl Harris with two of his children and one of several Ramblers that he owns.

Karl Harris is Principal Research and Development Engineer for II-VI Incorporated, an electro-optics materials and optics manufacturer whose products are used for a variety of visible, infrared, x-ray and gamma-ray applications. He has been involved with the AMC hobby since 1990. Karl wishes to thank his wife and family for their support through the many nights of sorting and restoring the Watson files that survived both fire and water damage. Although Karl has written numerous technical papers and reports, this is the first time he has contributed to a publication that people will read for pleasure.

Bibliography

American Motors Family Album, 1976 edition, by John A. Conde

Annual Report to the Stockholders of American Motors Corp. 1954-1962 editions

Autocar, March 26, 1954 issue

Automobile Topics, April 1960 issue

Car Life magazine, April 1955, January & August 1956 issues

Engineering Ventures in Personal Transportation - The Metropolitan. By W.S. Berry and L.H. Nagler, American Motors engineers. A paper delivered to The American Society of Body Engineers, February 17, 1955

Mechanics Illustrated, April 1954 issue

Motor, March 17, March 24, September 1, and October 27, 1954 issues, May 16, 1956 and April 3, 1957 issues

Motor Life magazine, July 1954 and August 1956 issues

Motorists magazine, July/August 1954 issue

Motor Trend magazine, May 1954, July 1954, January 1957 issues

Nash Family Album, 1956 edition

Popular Mechanics magazine, April 1954 issue

Popular Science, April 1954 issue

Road & Track, August 1954 issue

Special Interest Autos magazine, July 1971, July 1975 and May 1992 issues

Sports Car Illustrated magazine, May 1957 issue

The Met Letter - all issues

The Cars That Hudson Built, by John A. Conde, published 1980

The Story of George Romney, by Tom Mahoney, published 1960

What the Metropolitan Means to the Nash Dealer, Salesman and Owner, by James Watson, May 1954

In addition to the above, the author made use of thousands of Nash, Austin and AMC memos, notes, telegrams, speeches and letters as well as Product Information Reports, Product Analysis Reports, Data Books, Owners Manuals, Nash, Hudson, AMC and Austin Metropolitan sales brochures and service manuals, as well as production reports, sales reports and press releases, the listing of which in detail would require many pages that the author feels would not interest the average enthusiast.

Index

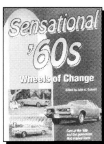

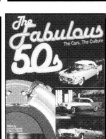
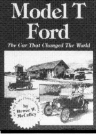

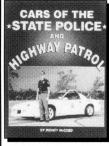

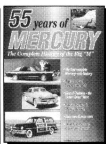
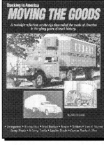
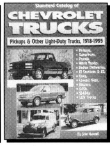

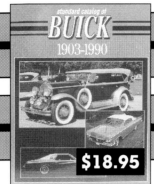
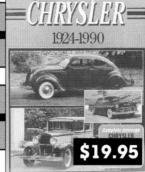
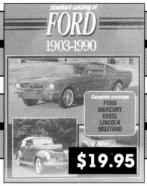

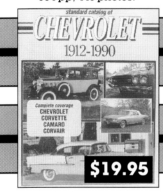

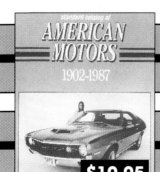